14/95

PLAYING FOR KEEPS

PLAYING FOR KEEPS

CLIFF THORBURN
with Clive Everton

PARTRIDGE PRESS

The author and publisher acknowledge photographs by Adonis Photo Studio, page 19; M. Athar Chaudhry, page 40; Thames Television, page 44; Terry Husband, page 48; Dave Muscroft, pages 60, 70, 73, 79, 98, 104, 119; White's News Agency, page 76; Guinness, page 88; Eric Whitehead, page 126.

Published in Great Britain by
Partridge Press
Maxwelton House
Boltro Road
Haywards Heath
West Sussex

(Partridge Press is an imprint of
Transworld Publishers Ltd, 61–63 Uxbridge Road,
London W5)

Typeset by Adlard & Son Ltd, The Garden City Press,
Dorking, Surrey

Printed and bound in Great Britain by
R.J. Acford, Chichester, Sussex

ISBN 1-85225-011-9

CONTENTS

AUTHOR'S PREFACE

I was lucky to find snooker when I did and lucky to be blessed with a talent for playing it. I was also lucky to be playing at the same time that snooker took off in a big way with television and sponsorship. If I had been the standard that I am in the 1950s, I would still have been one of the top players but I wouldn't have much money to show for it. The last ten years have been very good but the game still has a lot of strides to make world-wide and the 1990s are going to make the 1970s look like the 1950s.

Lots of people have asked me when I was going to write a book because they had found the stories I told interesting. I also thought it was about time that I said 'thank you' in a lasting way, in public, to the people who have helped me and maybe give a few insights about situations that won't have appeared in print before.

There's more to me than you can see or hear from watching me play on television. *Playing for Keeps* is to show how I became the player and the person that I am.

Cliff Thorburn

EDITOR'S NOTE

Cliff and I were both determined that *Playing for Keeps* would be his telling of his own story in his own words. Minus the ums and ers and shuffled into chronological order – though even Cliff is doubtful of this in places – the book reflects nearly 30 hours of taped conversations between us.

I have also included some comments of my own, either to set Cliff's career into context or simply to supplement his memory: these passages are clearly identifiable by change of typestyle. The use of some *Snooker Scene* match reports provides a fuller version of certain encounters for the snooker aficionado of how these matches looked at the time.

Clive Everton

INTRODUCTION

WHETHER CLIFF THORBURN wins a second world title or whether he achieves his only unfulfilled snooker ambition to reach No 1 in the rankings will have only a marginal effect on his reputation and status in the modern game. Not only because of his record but for the qualities he epitomises, he has become one of the giants of the game in the most exciting period of growth snooker has experienced.

World champion in 1980, second in the world rankings at the end of the 1985–6 season, he stood fourth at the point *Playing for Keeps* ends. He is the best non-British player there has ever been in a sport in which almost all the worthwhile tournament activity has always been in Britain, and non-British players have always had extra disadvantages to surmount.

He can expect another five years or so at the peak of his mature powers, possibly longer if he remains highly motivated. Some of his supporters fear that his sharpness of desire may be blunted by financial security and the easy-going satisfactions of family life with his wife, Barbara, and their two young sons, so different from the upbringing which, is some ways, was the making of him. His relish for battle in the arena, though, is undiminished and even if, as he grows older, he inevitably finds it more difficult to put himself through the necessary hours of practice, he has worked too hard to get where he is to give anything away without applying all the formidable self-discipline which is his trademark.

I have known Cliff since he first came to Britain for the 1973 world championship. He was all at sea with British conditions, but it was immediately obvious that he had a rare intensity and an implacable will to succeed. At that time, I knew nothing of his earlier life, of the grim struggle for moral, even physical, survival it had often been. It has since struck me how well Cliff has managed to harness to his advantage the kind of experience which would have crushed most.

Abandoned as a baby by his mother, the victim of a custody struggle which kept him in an orphanage until he left it to be brought up by his father and his father's mother, he was an inwardly solitary child, despite all the friends of his own age he made on the sports field. He could make little sense of the adult world, and instinctively suspected the attitudes and values of most adults with whom he came in contact. So he sought refuge in the world of sport, where inequalities of birth and wealth are at least minimised and where the rules and codes of the game impose a sense of order not to be found in the incoherence of 'real life'.

Perhaps, too, he had the rage of the abandoned even if it took years for this to dawn on him in full. At the age of 20, he learned that his mother had not died when he was a baby, as his father's side had always told him, but was in fact alive and well and living with the four children of her second marriage. He felt betrayed by their reluctance to treat him as an adult by not telling him the truth. As Cliff reveals, he simply tried harder to make something of himself.

In his early 20s, Cliff had only a hazy idea that there was even a world snooker championship and had no idea whatsoever about how to enter it or how to become a tournament professional. Instead, he was learning his trade in the toughest of schools, playing for keeps in the pool rooms of Canada and North America. Cliff learned how to play for keeps – whether it was nine ball against a fisherman who pulled a knife on him in Campbell River, pink ball in San Francisco in the days of Flower Power, the hippies and Sergeant Pepper, or snooker in Deli, Ontario, on a red cloth with 15 yellows instead of reds. He was prepared to lose his last $10 and not eat; he was prepared to take the other man's. Excuses and self-pity had no currency in these places and to this day Cliff does not indulge in either.

"I don't want this to seem as if I had a real tough deal because I didn't," he said to me as we were working on a section of the book when his life appeared to be hard going. "I was doing what I wanted to do. I was broke sometimes, or hungry or freezing cold but there was always another day."

He played eight to ten hours a day for ten years, making innumerable technical experiments, grooving his cue action so that it stayed straight and true under pressure. Always, he was distilling the experience of all these hours to make himself a better player. Often, his decision-making, his technique, his strength of mind has crystallised when he has most needed it to. At least twice, when he won the world title in 1980; and when, in 1983, he made the first 147 maximum break in the world championship, this crystallisation carried his performance on to the plane of inspiration which a competitor seeks all his life.

He will never be the darling of the fans because he is not a natural extrovert and because he was not born with the conspicuous talents of a Jimmy White or an Alex Higgins. He cannot play well without trying as the prodigiously gifted sometimes seem to. But as White once said: "Anyone who says Cliff is boring doesn't know anything about the game". Anyone who does know the game recognises his quality, his professionalism, his pride of performance, and above all, the lasting love for the game without which no player can go on functioning to the best of his ability. It is in Cliff's character that he will keep playing and that he will keep playing for keeps.

Clive Everton

ONE

SPORTS NUT

MY MOTHER and my father separated when I was about a year and a half. My mother didn't want to be with my father and my father didn't want me to be with my mother, so consequently I was just put in an orphanage for two years. I don't remember much about that except for this massive slide that went from the second floor down to the first floor. I was put into a couple of homes where people looked after me and I can remember that I got spanked with a wooden spoon because I went outside the gate. I guess I was about three or four.

So, finally, my grandmother, who was a very strong woman, got custody of me and I was raised by my grandmother and father. My grandmother was very strict yet my father was very loving towards me and let me get away with murder so to speak. My grandmother was the strong one, you see. Even so, she couldn't control me and I was sent to my Uncle Dave who had a couple of kids of his own, in Naniamo, British Columbia, for more strictness. I was five. Much later, but for the same reason, when I was about 11 or 12, I was sent away to my Uncle Bruce. He was what they used to call a good father. In other words, the sort where the kids grew up completely regimented.

He used to do six or seven hundred press-ups a day. He was that kind of guy. He was also into hypnotism. He hypnotised me once and said that when I woke up I was going to go into the kitchen and make myself a peanut butter sandwich. He must have been a better hypnotist than he thought. I went into the kitchen, but I actually had five peanut butter sandwiches. With the fifth, I threw up and the kitchen smelt of peanut butter for weeks.

My father didn't have much of an education. He was taken out of school by my aunts and uncles and my grandmother and grandfather, because they felt he was an

1

Left: My dad, my grandmother and me at home.

I'm on the right with my cousins at Uncle Clay's in Vancover.

The five year-old tearaway is on the left with my cousins Drew and Lynn at my Uncle Dave's in Naniamo

embarrassment to the family. My dad is a bit nervous and when he talks, he talks very quickly.

I've got a lot of him in me. When I was 11 or 12, we all had to stand up once a week in reading class, or whatever it was, to recite something from a book. When I got to a certain point, like a word with a sound like o, ah, aye, I couldn't say it so I just packed in reading. Consequently, I grew up with no direction in life. I hated school. I got kicked out of three, not for being really bad but just for being mischievous or whatever. I didn't like the system.

I passed my first eight years in school but then I went to Grade 9 and I had no interest at all. I started to play truant, I failed Grade 9 so I went back for another year. We had this teacher, Peter Dawes, who had been a Rhodes Scholar at Oxford. He was real tough, the hardest teacher you would ever want to meet. At the end of the year he gave the whole class their report cards, except for me. He told me to stay behind. So I know I've failed. I didn't care. So he said to me that I'd failed again, but "I've passed you because I don't wanna see your goddam face in school any more".

So now I had to go back to Grade 10 and I started to play truant again. My grandmother would come in at 8 o'clock in the morning with her cane and whack me around the shoulders: "Get up. Get up". On days like that I would go to school but then I wouldn't go for maybe three or four days. The truant officer would stop by for a coffee and ask me why I didn't want to go to school. He got into such a routine that he'd come to our place for a cup of coffee about 9.30 or 10 o'clock every morning.

One day I'm down in the basement chopping some wood. We start talking and he says: "Here, give me the axe". I thought it was kinda funny that he was my truant officer and here he was chopping my wood for me. Anyway, in the end he said: "Cliff, I know you're not school material, but you've got a good mind so go out and do what you want. But if you do find something, make sure you stick with it." This meant a lot to me at the time.

The other thing I remember from school was my swimming teacher. I was born a mile from the water and I lived even nearer, but I was really skinny as a kid so I never used to go down to the beach because there was no way I would take my shirt off. I couldn't swim so when I was 10 or 11 I went to the swimming class. I was very nervous and this teacher finally just pushed my head under the water. I went down with my mouth wide open and I could see the bubbles going up until her face disappeared. That finished me. I still can't swim, although I have had various people try to teach me.

Apart from sports, the best thing I remember about my very young days was Mrs Austin and her cookies. There were six or seven of us boys who were all sports nuts who would go over to her house. Her son, Les, was a friend of mine and I spent more time there than I did in my own house. Mrs Austin would make some cookies and I can't tell you how good they were. She was like a mother to me.

When I was young, I used to climb out of the bedroom window when they thought that I was asleep and I'd play ball games with the older kids. I had it down to a complete science. My grandmother and father absolutely believed that I was asleep and I'd be up on the street playing baseball. I'd sneak back in through the front door, but one night the front door was locked and that was the end of that.

We used to play a game called scrub baseball. We'd all go home from school for an hour's lunchbreak – I lived about a five-minute run away – and we'd all rush back. The first person back got to be the batter, second guy was the catcher, third was the pitcher, fourth was first base and so on. I remember how excited I used to be to get lunch over with and be first back so that I'd have the bat. I was a good enough hitter that I could actually stay out the whole lunch hour, but once you were in the outfield, the buzzer might ring and you'd never get to bat.

One time, I ate lunch and wolfed this banana down so that I could be first back. I had got to the goalpost where the baseball field was and I had so much banana in my mouth that I started choking. I passed out. I woke up and was still the first one there. It could have been all over! I was all by myself so I was lucky.

My father pushed me into sports and being the type of man that he is he probably got more satisfaction out of my life than his own. He doesn't really say that much to me and he wasn't the type for me to run home and give him a hug or anything like that. It just wasn't done because he was ruled by my grandmother because of this thing in the past. But we understood each other.

He ended up being my coach at soccer, basketball and baseball. Anything to be involved with sports. He was like that because when he was 10 or 11 he had a very serious appendicitis and he wasn't really allowed to be too active. I know for a fact that I was what he wanted to be and that he really saw in me truly an extension of him. As time went on, he could obviously see the talent that I had.

When I was seven or eight years old he was still keeping scrapbooks of the Montreal Canadians hockey team. He was just so involved with sports, although he never really understood it. He loved the great players of sports and was always reminding me all the time of Mickey Mantle, the famous baseball player, or Rocket Richard at hockey. He was always talking about them and I was wide-eyed and bushy-tailed. All that is still inbred with me. I've got a New York Yankees hat which I wear just walking down the street or just having fun.

I had the same teammates in every single sport and he'd run us all around. The great thing about North American life is that there are so many things that you could actually have a shot at in your life. There were so many ways out. I guess I played snooker because I knew that I wasn't going to be good enough at all the other things I tried, although I was exceedingly better than average. My body wasn't proportioned properly for those games so I grew up tall and thin. Finally, I couldn't throw a baseball hard enough to be good at the age of 16 or 17 or else I'd get cross-checked at lacrosse.

My father had a lot to do with my personal development. I still don't understand him. I do in a way but I don't. I'm sure most sons don't understand their fathers. When I was about 10, I was playing baseball in the park and I was really getting excited about it. I'm another Babe Ruth; nobody can tell me different. And I had to play this game of lacrosse that morning and you have to appreciate that lacrosse in Victoria BC is our national sport, more than ice hockey. My dad wanted me to play lacrosse but I was really getting fed up with it. My dad said that I had to play and I didn't want to, so he chased me all around the park.

I had a game at ten o'clock, but I'm at the baseball park at 8 am and we're into it. So my dad finally dragged me into the car and we start to drive to the game which had referees and all that and the results were in the papers with a little story. Halfway there we stopped at a stop sign, so I bolted. Door open, gone. So then my dad's got my lacrosse stick and he's chasing me and he said I must play. Finally, I've got up a tree, and he's trying to climb up and he's whacking me on the feet with this stick because he's upset. That day I scored ten goals, which was a record.

I saw something different in my father that day. I saw the goodness probably for the first time. I didn't think of how he felt or how proud he was or anything like that. I just saw something there that I'd never seen before. I guess then I knew I had some direction.

School and living at home – except for my father – was like being in the army. It was so regimented. I was so into sports and games and balls and spin on the ball that I had no time for anything else – I mean *anything* else – and it felt like I was in the army and I just had to get out of it.

I didn't understand it. I didn't understand the meaning of an education when I can look at the world, look at the water and just look at all the beautiful things in life. I couldn't see any meaning for education and I couldn't face going back home at night to something I didn't understand, didn't enjoy unless my father and I were talking about sports.

It was as if I wanted to get out of the real world. A board game that I bought was based on the 16 teams in the major baseball leagues. Each team played 20 times or maybe 23 or 24 times. Each team had 20 players, each player had his own separate card and there were dice numbers on it up to 66. There is a computer telling what each guy's batting average was at, whether he's playing Grade A, B or C and so on. It was fantastically complex and I couldn't have had more entertainment value for my money. I played a full league programme, which is about 162 games. I was totally gone and my son, who's six, is like the way that I was in that if he's watching something that he likes you can't penetrate to him. You have to shake him. My dad's the same. If he's involved with something, you just can't get into his head at all. He blanks out everything except what he's concentrating on.

Also around this time, I used to play golf. Two friends of mine, Smitty – his real name was Bob Smith – and his next-door neighbour Doug Metters, arranged little putt-putt course around his mother's house. We had the holes and we smoothed out the fairways with a lawnmower. We had 18 holes and for us it was like something that you see on TV. "Four under after six," we'd holler.

We'd also play roller hockey with a tennis ball and two nets each side of the street. We'd play till long past dark. None of us could wait to get out of school each day. The only thing that kept us going at school was firing spit balls at the ceiling. We'd take a piece of paper, roll it up, put it in our mouth, make it nice and juicy and fire it at the ceiling with a ruler. Eventually, there were three or four hundred of these things stuck to the ceiling.

I remember playing in the BC baseball championships at the age of 12 where we played a team that beat us and went to the junior world series in Williamsburg, Pennsylvania. It's televised around the world. It's just unbelievable how big Little League baseball is. The morning before I was scheduled to pitch I went out and played lacrosse. I was completely whacked out and we lost the game 22–8 and this team went on the Little League world series. We had a team basically of misfits, scrubbers, but I'm convinced to this day that if I hadn't gone out and played lacrosse that we would have been where this team went because we were as polished and as talented. They got eight runs off me in the first inning and I went out to the outfield and I bawled my eyes out. I'd left the bases loaded. I went out to

The James Bay Little League baseball team. I'm second from left

centre field and the next guy up first pitch hit it right over my head for a home run and now we're losing by 12–0. It was devastating.

Then, when I was 15, I was the No 1 pitcher for the Babe Ruth team playing in the BC championships in my home town and the team that beat us 1–0 in one extra innings went to Albuquerque, New Mexico, for the Babe Ruth world series. I thought I pitched pretty good, then I threw a wild pitch that went past the catchers. So the guy on first went to second, and then there was a ground ball into the short stop and he missed it. Finally, there was a player at the plate and the catcher dropped it, and we had lost. The tears. All in the dug-out crying our eyes out and we're all 15 or 16. And then I knew that team sports weren't for me because I wasn't talented enough to be able to do it by myself. A pitcher who was going to get to the major leagues wouldn't have thrown the pass ball.

Like I say, I have a lot of my father in me and it's had a great bearing on my life, not only in being competitive but simply in how I was at home. I couldn't really have a conversation, a proper father and son type of conversation, because my dad

6

is a very, very nervous type of person. He was regarded as the black sheep of the family but, when I got older and started playing snooker well, then I became the black sheep of the family. Until I was 20 or so I was always trying to get away from this stigma that was attached to my father and myself. I wanted to prove something to my father. I wanted him to know what I thought of him. But there I was trying to get away from one stigma and I walked into another, the stigma of being a pool player.

I was an outsider and, of course, when I came over to England much later I was an outsider again, partly through being a Canadian among all the Brits and also through my style of play. I've always been trying to get away from something that I've never really understood. I've been constantly trying to prove myself.

I always had much better than average eye-to-hand co-ordination. I always knew what was relevant in games, like the effects a ball spinning will have. I still think to this day that if I'd paid more attention to my own personal body development, working out and getting stronger, that I probably could have been a professional lacrosse player. There's not much money in it, but I might have stayed with that and been very, very happy.

I had visions of being a professional baseball player and I was asked to go to the Kansas City Royals centre for a trial in my home town. My dad knew that I was good. I knew that I was good. I wasn't a strong physical type of person, but I did have a lot of moxy. I can't straighten my right arm now because I threw so many curved balls.

But I could feel myself weakening physically. I was 16. I couldn't keep up with the chaps that were better built than me. But for this, I knew that I could have handled myself, because I had the ability, if the ball was coming, to make a split-second decision. That may sound odd to some people who watch me play snooker, but I know most of the time what I'm going to do right away. What sometimes slows me up is that I see a lot of different ways to go but now I'm so experienced that these decisions have become much easier.

I don't shoot until I'm ready and I'm getting ready quicker. I'm probably the most successful poor form player there's ever been because I've been used to fighting for survival all the time. I take calculated risks and that has made me what I am today, although I probably have taken more risks and played more stupid shots in the last couple of years than I had in all my snooker career before.

I knew that I was going to be good at something. I was born with that. Sport is such a lovely thing and all the people out there who've never been competitive have missed out on life in general. I watched Canada play England in women's hockey and loved it. I love to watch rugby over here. I played soccer for nine years. I was a goalkeeper and I loved it. I played Tony Knowles at tennis in Australia and I was so upset when I lost.

I visualise. When I won the championship, I saw myself holding that trophy up before I won it. I saw myself make a 147 break in the world championship before I made it. I saw it as clear, probably even clearer than when it did actually happen. I've been striving for the moment and when it happens it's not as good as it could be. But you go on striving.

I could name eight or ten of my good friends at that time who went the wrong way in life. I could name two that died in jail from drug overdoses, and various other people who were casual acquaintances of mine that ended up dying from drugs. I never had to fight that type of urge, but if I had been just a little bit weaker there's no telling.

But with sports and games there was a light there and I never really got off the track. I just followed it all along because I yearned to be involved with sport even if at the end of it I was the guy that carried the water bucket.

TWO

ON THE ROAD

MY DAD took me bowling one night when I was 10 or 11. I heard the click of pool balls coming from the floor below and decided to take a look. It was game for money, a crowd getting excited. In the end there was a big groan when one guy banked (doubled) the eight ball in the side pocket to win. I just knew then that I wanted to be part of it all, becoming a man and all that stuff.

The winner was a guy called Ernie Jay. Another guy stepped out of the crowd and slammed his money down on the table. I was spotted. "Hey, who's that kid?" I beat it back up the stairs.

As I was growing up, I caught glimpses of a few games like that from time to time, but I was busy with my own sport until I was well into my teens. Snooker was about the only game my father didn't want me to play. There was a kind of stigma on being a pool player or a snooker player because the good players were regarded as just hustlers – conmen – and most of the pool halls were pretty rough places.

When I was about 16 I had a good friend who was always in trouble with the police. He'd been hanging round the pool rooms for about a year and this day I went in with him. I learned my first lesson. He said we should play best of three at eight ball, loser pays for the table. I won 2–1 and he says why don't we make it the best of five. So we go on and on until after about 27 games he's ahead and he says: "Right, that's enough" and goes leaving me stuck to pay $10 for the table. I only had $2 in my pocket so I end up my first game of pool being kicked out the pool hall.

I paid that off but another time I went to the same pool hall and found after I'd been playing for a while that I'd forgotten my money. "OK, you can owe me the dollar," the guy says but then there's some mumbling from somewhere else that I'd been barred from the hall for not paying. About five years later, just after I'd won the Canadian Championship, I went back and gave the man his dollar.

"Thanks," he said, "but you're still barred."

As soon as I quit school at 16, I packed in all athletic-type games. After a year and a half playing snooker in Victoria I was the best player in town. Ernie Jay had been the best player for years and for about three months I played him a dollar a game. He must have won $100 dollars off me. Then, one day, we played best of five. It was 2–2. Then in the fifth I cleared up the last six reds and the colours.

He just said: "That's enough, Cliff. You're too good for me." My friends thought I was crazy losing $100 to this man and then beating him for just one dollar, but I was so happy.

My father kept saying I should get myself a regular job but after leaving school I never had one for more than a few weeks. The first I ever had was delivering "fliers" – advertising stickers – saying: "Smith's super sale opens today" and stuff like that.

I took a trip up to Campbell River and played Len Homenchuk, who was the first good player I'd seen. I started to see the strategy of the game and value of being round the black.

Campbell River is a kind of fishing village on Vancouver Island and at about the same time I took another trip up there. I probably played the best pool of my life that day, but I just picked the wrong guy. I beat him about seven games in a row and the fellow called me a hustler. The guy pushed me and I smacked him on the shoulder. I had learnt at school that the first punch in a fight is the most important. Then I backed up a bit; then he went to go at me again, and then he pulled out this knife with a jagged edge. I started to run. The fellow cut me off. Then it was stopped. If somebody hadn't stepped in and said the right thing who knows what would have happened.

I was always wanting to go into town and play and sometimes I even had to steal a little bit of money off my father to do it. Once, with one of my friends, a guy called Danny, who was living with my granny, we cashed her old age pension cheque. There was $70 there for two weeks. I took it. I left town and when I came back I just thoroughly denied it to my grandmother and my father. Looking back, they were great about it but they knew and I knew that they knew but I couldn't say that I did. So to this day, because of that, I won't take advantage of anybody. If, say, I was with Bill Werbeniuk and we made $201, he got $101. That's my repentance.

Anyway, with that $70 I went with a friend of mine, Bob Montgomery, to Vancouver to play John Bear, who was the best player in town. He's a full-blooded Indian and much later turned professional, but he didn't go too much for life on the tournament circuit and dropped out. His brother Jim, also a very good player, reached the final of the world amateur in Calgary in 1982 and now plays the professional circuit. I beat him in the 1987 Canadian Professional Championship final.

At that time, John just played around Vancouver. He never left town because he didn't need to. When I showed up to play him he put me through very nicely. He gave me 10, 20, 30, 40, up to 60 and took all my money. And he did it so nicely that even when he had all my money I still thought what a nice guy he was. He gave me $10 to get home, but the next time I headed out of Victoria I went right by Vancouver. I didn't play him again until about 1970. By that time we both knew he couldn't beat me.

So I went back to Victoria with my tail between my legs. I felt really cooped up there. Victoria's on an island so you feel like you can't get out. I couldn't handle it. I would have got into real trouble if it hadn't been for snooker. I got into enough trouble as it was. A guy called Dave Smith kept a place called the Cue and Cushion. You rented a cue for 50 cents a month and you stuck it up on the wall in a case. The first cue I had, I just broke in frustration, just snapped it, and I didn't know where to put it. I just happened to notice a hole in the stairwell which was covered by a board so I put it behind there and then put my name tag on another cue. Anyway in time, I broke about ten cues and the guy must have started wondering by this time where all these cues were going.

One day, Dave puts his head in this hole and there's 12 Thorburn cues all shattered. He was kinda upset and I was barred.

Then he went on holiday and this guy filled in for him so I bluffed my way in again. As you can tell from all the broken cues, I got a little wild when I missed shots that I thought I should be getting. This time, I missed a black and I'm so upset I just picked it up and threw it at the wall. The wall was made of some soft stuff so the black just stuck in there. I was trying to get it out and the guy who let me in spots me. I ask can I borrow his screwdriver, but when he sees what I want to borrow it for he goes crazy and rams me against the wall. So I got booted out of there.

Soon after that I met a guy whose name was Rose, I think, and he asked me if I wanted to go to Calgary. It was 640 miles. We managed to hitch-hike as far as a place called Suffield, which was where his mother lived. We got dropped off at Rose's place around two in the morning. It was 30 degrees below zero. I was wearing a tee shirt and a rain-jacket. At the door, his folks said straight away that I couldn't stay there. Rose decided to stay home with his parents. I turned back to the highway one and a half miles away, just in my tee shirt and rain-jacket, and waited for a car or truck to come along.

I guess that my life started right there and then standing out there on the highway by myself. I didn't know where east or west was and it was pitch dark. I got lucky and I went straight east from there. I can't tell you how cold I was. I was cold to the marrow, almost bent double. I was 17 and I didn't know enough to realise just how young that was. I got picked up by three guys so I was lucky not only because I got picked up because there was no trouble.

They took me all the way to Yorktown, Saskatchewan. I was broke so I went to the police station and they sent me to the Salvation Army hostel for a week with all the rummies and the hoboes. Then I went to a pool room and made $100 and that took me on to Winnipeg. I finished up broke there, too, which meant it was back to the Salvation Army until I could make a few more dollars for myself by gambling. I used to get breakfast there about 7.30 and then I'd go across the street to a place called Fox Billiards. Snooker was ten cents a game and sometimes I'd get down to the pink or something and start playing snookers to make the game last longer.

Then I met a chap who had the inside word on a freight train going to Toronto. I knew that George Chenier had a billiard room in Toronto and I wanted to see this guy I'd heard so much about. He'd had a room in Victoria years earlier and they still talked about him with total awe. A little guy named Ezra, who wore a green eyeshade and glasses, swore he never saw him miss a ball in five years. Time and again I was told that he just never missed. I made some allowance for exaggeration but still I figured that this man I had to see. So the idea was for my friend and I to

George Chenier, the Canadian and North American champion who was Canada's first world class snooker player. He's pictured here before the start of his 1950 world quarter-final against Peter Mans, Perrie's father, at Scunthorpe

hop on this freight train going from Winnipeg to Toronto. We perched ourselves in the fourth or fifth engine. The train was about 100 box cars long and it needed all those engines to get up the hills.

At one of the stops my friend said we should get some food so we went to a store and pinched a nutcake. As a matter of fact there were three nutcakes – my friend and I and the cake. We'd been on the train for about two and a half days, not daring to look out because of the Canadian Pacific police, when suddenly we were in a place called Smith Falls. I heard people talking French. This told me we weren't where we should have been. Although I didn't know it at the time, we were already 200 miles east of Toronto – and going east. When we got to Montreal I knew it was time to bale out.

I'd been travelling so long on this train, it doesn't look like it's going fast at all so we decided to hop off. I really thought it was going about five miles an hour and it was probably doing 25. I jumped well clear. I thought I'd be able to step off daintily but of course I'm going as fast as the train. I turned to get my balance and I went spreadeagled, feet out, and by that time I'm a missile. I bounced and hit the ground in thick mud. I was already covered in soot from the engine so after I'd hit the ground and rolled for 25 yards or so in thick mud I looked like Sambo.

We had to find our way out of the railway yard and we were worried about the CP police. The way we looked it was amazing that anybody ever gave us a lift, but this guy did. He said: "Holy cow, are you guys in bad shape". We told him we hadn't eaten and we hadn't – nothing except the nutcake. I can still feel the taste in my mouth when I think about it. Talk about bad breath! Talk about putrid! This fella gave us $20 and dropped us off in Montreal. When I saw myself for the first time I couldn't believe the guy had let us in his car. It was a nice car and I look like I had come out of a mine. Also, $20 then is probably worth about $60 today so we were very lucky that night.

The money this guy had given me got me somewhere to stay for the night, a coat and a new pair of pants. The hotel was about two or three dollars a night but after about three days I couldn't pay my hotel bill so they kept my clothes as security. I went back about four years later to pick them up. I couldn't believe I had actually bought the stuff.

My friend and I split up in Montreal. I was able to live just by playing for quarters and dimes. I picked my spots just to earn some money. Playing for 25 cents in a bad part of town was how you grew up.

Then I went to this place called the Windsor Bowling Alley which was very famous because that's where Leo Levitt played. There was a plaque on the wall about his 147. I hung around there for about three days because he worked in a car dealership. I was waiting to see him play but he never did actually show up. There were some pictures of Eddie Agha there, too, but I didn't see him play on this trip either. I never actually saw any of the top players although I'm convinced I might have played a few at the time without knowing who they were.

I met Leo a couple of years later. He was a fun player more or less. He played for a couple of dollars or five dollars, something like that, but he couldn't play to his best standard in a real match. I have to say, though, that he made his 147 on a very

Eddie Agha

13

tough table, an old Brunswick Monarch with quite small pockets. Leo was OK. He smoked a cigar and always wore a hat. He was drowned a few years ago when his boat overturned while he was out fishing.

My money was depreciating quite considerably when I got the chance of a ride to Toronto. To this day, I've never been to Toronto so fast. The guy was doing 110 miles an hour all the way. I hung around in Toronto for about a month just so that I could see Chenier play.

I went in one place called Plaza Billiards, which isn't there now. There was one chap there who bet on the horses a lot. He was really smooth. He smoked cigars and he played with the looped bridge. People would come up to him every couple of hours and say: "Wanna play?" He'd say "yes" and he'd beat everybody. I could see his bankroll increasing all the time and I thought: "Christ, what a wonderful way to live." I was almost like a fly on the wall. I didn't dream of asking this guy with the cigar to play.

I learned a lot then. All the heroes among the people I saw then had a tough guy act: pan-faced, don't-smile, can't-figure- this-guy-at-all. That worried most people and that was what I had to do. That's what I became and it was very successful for me. I can have lots of fun when I'm not playing snooker, but when I'm playing I find it very hard not to be very serious.

Finally I ran Chenier to earth in a pool hall called the Golden Mile. When I walked in this place he was just clearing the last three reds, with blacks, nothing spectacular, but there was something in the way he cued, the way he hit the ball. It was the first time I had seen class. I just melted. It turned me on to the way he played and I decided right there that that was how I wanted to play. He wasn't slow but if he needed to spend a while studying the shot and getting his head together, he did. He was quite old and sick by then and he didn't have much cue power, but I already knew that the guys who powered the ball lost their money every single day.

Later, much later, I came to know him. He was one of the nicest guys I ever met and he gave me and many other people a lot of help. He only came to England once and it's a great pity that he didn't come more often but he hated the politics of the game and he felt cheated when the 144 he made wasn't recognised as a world record. Just after that Joe Davis made a 146 and that was ratified. As George stormed out of the Control Council offices, he said: "You and the ----ing Americans are exactly the same. You're both full of bullshit but at least the Americans can back it up."

One of the curious things about him was that he was colour blind and he had to be very careful about distinguishing the brown from the reds. He stood much more upright than a snooker player does these days, peering over the tip rather than looking down the shaft of the cue, a pool player's stance in fact rather than a snooker player's.

That night in Toronto, though, I was just another kid passing through. About the third game he made a 127. I would never have dreamt of speaking to him. I just wouldn't have known what to say. Around that time I'd be a 35 or 40 break player, but I was surviving and I was seeing the country one way or another. I knew how much it cost to get from A to B. I knew how much a hotel room was. I knew how much a good meal was.

When I finally got back to Victoria, I lived with a girl called Cheryl Ferguson. She had a 53 Chev, a bright red one. She was a big girl, a solid girl: she looked after me. I lived with her and I used to go and play snooker. Around about that time I made a 65. I washed dishes on the Victoria–Seattle shuttle to get a night in Seattle playing for money.

When I was about 18 or 19, I had a real good trip when I finally ended up in Sudbury with fellows like Gabe Tarini and Roger Frenette. Because of all the nickel mines there were a lot of Frenchmen there gambling. They played snooker, but they played points, sometimes known as "shellouts". I used to love watching them play and finally I got to be good enough to get in the game. I lived there for about three or four months.

I had this friend called Mo La Plante. We were in this band. I was the lead singer and we weren't bad. We did a couple of gigs, but the other three guys in the band went to jail for breaking and entering so that was the end of that. We were called the Sticks, not to be confused with another group called Styx, which was around the time of the Beatles and the Stones. Mo would go back to his house because he was married. I'd stop at a boarding house. We'd go walking down the road singing at the top of our lungs and people would be shouting "Shut up" or "I'm gonna phone the police". I had a real high voice and Mo had a high voice and we sounded pretty good to ourselves. I wasn't breaking the law and I was doing the two things that I really loved, singing and playing snooker. I was picking up things about snooker all the time and I couldn't wait to get to the hall next day. Nine o'clock first thing, I'd be there thinking: "What the hell's he doing? Where is he?" Finally, the guy would show up and I'd say: "Gee, where've you been?" Don McFadden was another specially good friend I had in Sudbury.

I'd play all day. I'd play for 14 hours solid and there were some characters around. There was one guy called Gabby from Sturgeon Falls. He had one eye but, boy, could this guy pot. He also became the world wrist-wrestling champion. Two or three years later I ended up playing him in Toronto, just the blue off its spot and the cue ball on the baulk line, $5 a hit. I made 19 out of 20 and lost $5.

He was playing a guy once when he potted the black to win the frame and then decided to go to the toilet. He pulled his eye out, stuck it on the table and said to someone: "Keep an eye on this guy while I'm gone."

Gabby was an exceptional guy, a hot-head in a way. Once, he said that if he missed this black he'd buy everybody in the place a Coca Cola. So now he's missed it and he has to order up 25 cokes. He opens up the first one, pours it down the drain and does that to every one.

He went up to a young kid once, who'd have been about sixteen or seventeen, and said: "Lend me $20."

"I'm not sure," the kid says, but then Gabby starts to threaten him and the kid says: "OK."

So Gabby sticks a match to it and says: "That'll teach you to lend me $20."

In Sturgeon Falls once he was playing this car dealer and he missed the black, which was for $400. He said to the guy at the counter: "How much are these cues?" The guy tells him $5. He broke 20 cues and then he gave the guy $100 and walked out. He was very easily distracted. Once he missed the black and looked right across the room where there was a guy in a bright red Hawaiian shirt just playing a game. He went across and just dropped the guy flat. He said: "Don't you ever wear that kind of shirt in here again". He was pretty dangerous, stronger than an ox, but when I'm shooting a blue off the spot from the baulk line I often think of him. I run that shot about 65 to 75 per cent right now.

I can't put my travels in much kind of order, but I was having a lot of fun. I was a young kid, naive, bright eyed and bushy-tailed. It was all new to me. I'd go wherever there was a chance to go.

I remember staying in a place in Vancouver for a while. There were four or five of us and we did nothing but play and talk snooker. I can remember going up and down the highway in the pouring rain with my two-piece cue and to this day people who didn't know me then say that they used to go by me on the highway in their cars laughing at me. I worked on a garbage truck for three months. It's the only thing in my life I was ever fast at.

I made my first century, 104, in Sudbury. I had been getting up to 80, 85 quite a lot but every time I did I felt as if I was having a heart attack. I decided that the next time I got to 80 I would play the balls as if I'd scored 20. Right away, I made a century.

Just after that I heard about Paul Thornley who had just won the Canadian championship. Chenier wasn't in it and although Paul could probably have beaten him by then he had so much respect for him, and for what he had done, that he wouldn't play him. To this day you can't have much of a conversation with Paul without him bringing Chenier's name into the conversation.

Toronto was about 260 miles away and I took the bus down there with Mo just to see Paul play. I saw him play a guy called Donny Reeves who had the same sort of short stroke action as Higgins. I happen to think that this is the best sort of action to have. Jimmy White, for instance, is like John Spencer, with that long backswing. John has said to me many times that if you're playing badly you should always try

Paul Thornley – and his loop bridge

16

to play the same, but I don't think this works, not for me anyway. Perhaps losing isn't all that big a deal to John and that has been to his detriment, I think. But losing is a big deal if you're playing without much money in your pocket so the best thing to do, I think, if you're playing badly, is to cut down your backswing to only a couple of inches and start from there just to get going.

Donny was a great potter, probably as good knocking a ball down a cushion as Davis or Higgins and he had terrific cue power. Paul Thornley played with a pool player's loop bridge with the finger tucked underneath. All the keen players in Toronto were playing like this and I tried it as well. It still comes in useful at times. Paul was playing very well and he really impressed me with the way he could pot the blue half ball into the middle pocket and take the cue ball into baulk and back out again. I must have practised that shot for three hours that night.

Paul was and is a very laid back character and knows as much about snooker as a game as any man alive. Something happened to his own game in the Seventies. His cue action would just freeze up every so often so when he did get to play in competitions he didn't do much. But at the time he was probably the best player in Canada. He was a very good money player and used to like crazy bets. He once beat somebody for some money playing with a coathanger.

About five years after I first met him I had this great idea that he should give me 70 start and I would play every shot with the rest, even if I was on the cushion. I beat him for a few dollars and I made an 85 break, just playing with the rest. For somebody who could have done that, I'm a bad rest player now.

There was another player around from Winnipeg called John Cassidy, or Doc Cassidy, who had an incredibly long backswing, beautiful to watch. He held his cue like a violin player holds his bow. His long backswing was his downfall, but he was still a pretty good player. Once I was standing there with my arms crossed just watching him play, just moving my body this way or that according to which direction I expected the cue ball to go. Then he played one shot where the cue ball had so much side on it that I expected it to go one way and I almost fell over with my own body movement when it went the other. People must have thought I was drunk or something.

One day, I went broke again. Mo knew Paul, and I went up to Paul and asked if I could borrow $10. He lent me the ten and said: "Don't worry about it". It was one of the nicest things that anybody had ever done for me. It made a very long lasting impression on me.

In the next few years I went across Canada and back about ten times, getting better all the time. I'd give somebody a start, say 20, win, go all the way across Canada, come back and then give them 30. Nobody could believe that I was getting that much better every single time. They probably thought that I was hustling them, but I wasn't. I was just getting better.

One of the places I kept going back to was Jake Feasel's in Regina, Saskatchewan. I remember, particularly, Henry Belrose and Jim Sinclair, who worked for the Canadian government in the Department of Indian Affairs.

Coming back from Toronto once, I was on the train to Vancouver, which is a journey which takes about 72 hours. I had about $10 to last me the three days on the train. We got to a place called Thunder Bay which I knew from my travels had a pool hall which sold the best steamed hot dogs I've ever had in my life. The train stopped for about an hour so I ran to this pool room and got two steamed hot dogs.

17

They'd be about 20 cents each. I was quite hungry. I smothered them with mustard and onions and wolfed them down. I asked the fellow behind the counter if he knew somebody who wanted to gamble. He nodded towards a guy in the corner who looked just perfect. He had the thickest glasses I've ever seen in my life, just like the bottom of a pop bottle. He had an old tee shirt on and some farmer's jeans with the straps. His boots, his wellies, were completely caked with cow shit, about three or four years of it, I would guess.

"Excuse me, sir . . . gamble . . . \$5 . . ."

He didn't hear me. He was deaf as well, but eventually we played for \$5. The game started to take a bit longer than I thought it would and the train only stopped for an hour. I knew that if it was close and I lost I'd only have \$5 to last me the rest of the journey because there wouldn't be time for another game. I could see myself eating nothing but cream crackers and things like that for 2,000 miles.

Anyway, the guy beats me. I'm devastated. I've only got 20 minutes now so I say to him: "Excuse me. Do you mind if we take some of the red balls off the table?" I kept saying "less red balls, less red balls" and this guy kept putting his hand to his ear because he couldn't hear what I was saying.

"Les who?" he said.

"No, no, less red balls, less red balls."

Eventually, he said "Les Red Balls? Never heard of him. Bring him on. I'll beat him, too." There was just no way I could get through to anyone who thought I was trying to steer him on to somebody else called Les Red Balls, so I went the rest of the way to Vancouver on \$5. I didn't gain too much weight around that time.

On one of my trips I stayed in Vancouver for about six months. I got to know all the guys involved with Bill Werbeniuk who I'd first met through his brother. His brother was talking about snooker in a disco and saying that Bill could beat me. I played Bill in a money match and he beat me 10–4. Then I beat him 10–1 or 10–2 the next two times we played.

Bill's dad, Shorty, was a hell of a character. He was Canadian champion before there was ever an official Canadian championship and obviously Bill absorbed a lot from him at an early age. Shorty was the original grinder. He was actually called The Grinder. This nickname never really stuck to me until Higgins called me by this name after I'd beaten him in the 1980 world final.

When Bill shook my hand before our first match he said: "You know, my dad always told me this".

And I said: "What?"

He said: "That anybody who's got sweaty hands has got brain damage".

Bill just overpowered me.

Eric Connelly was playing really well then. Every day he made at least a 135. We all learned a lot from him, but I think I learned more than Bill did because Bill couldn't mix the two styles. Eric had great control and touch, whereas Bill's natural style was power shots and long potting. He lacked finesse so he didn't want to get into the tight positional play that Eric had. But he would go for anything.

It was hard to explain to people in England just how well Eric was playing around 1966–7. He was from Newcastle originally. Then he lived in Birmingham and although he did quite well in some of the amateur tournaments nobody marked him up as anything exceptional. Then he went out to Canada. He was involved in some sort of business, but it didn't stop him playing five or six hours a

Top: Little Bill Werbeniuk. Later he became Big Bill Werbeniuk
Eric Connelly, who was playing some great snooker in Vancouver in the late Sixties

day so maybe that's why his reputation in Canada was a lot higher than it was in England. Eric's big dream was to own a snooker club and around 1984, back in Newcastle, he did. The morning after it opened, he was found dead from a heart attack.

Pender Billiards was the best room in Vancouver at the time. All the businessmen were there, plus Connelly and Werbeniuk. In those kind of places in those days you always had a racker. When you finished a game this guy would come round and take your 25 cents or whatever. When you finished a game, you'd just yell "Rack" and this guy, Wally, would appear to re-rack the balls and bring you sandwiches or whatever.

I had several spells in Vancouver, but, as a player, you can't last unless you travel. I also liked to move around. Anyway, one of the guys I met in Vancouver, Ike Pauls, I met again in Thunder Bay. We spent about two days together playing snooker and going out for a drink and he kept saying what a terrible place Thunder Bay was to be in. So I said: "Why don't we go to Toronto?" Ike was a barber but he just quit and we got a train to Toronto.

We met up with Steve Bosiak, who I'd got to know the first time I was there. Ike and I moved in with him. Steve would do his six or seven hours of work at night or during the day and I used to love the nights when we used to sit around at his place, drink some beer and talk snooker – strokes, this kind, that kind, this player, that player. They were into it as much as I was. I've never had more fun than that. It was so good for my mind and for my game and I wouldn't be where I am today if I hadn't done it.

One of the characters around Toronto then was a guy called The Whale, who made Bill Werbeniuk look like a baby. When this guy missed a ball, he would run straight at a wall with his head. Or he would get two balls in his hand and bang them against his head. Try that sometime. It hurts.

There was another guy, Mike Baker, who, when he would miss a ball, would get up on the table and start to ram his head into the pocket to show how big the pocket really was. Once, he was playing me and he missed the black for $50. He just stood there and said: "Godzilla's creation" and just let himself fall straight backwards flat on his back.

Another time, we were playing for $50 and he's missed the black to lose the game. Just beside the table, there's a pinball machine. He's walked up to it and he's punched it with his right hand – his bridge hand – about three or four times. The machine is solid wood. So then he says: "Let's play for a hundred" and I say "Sure". As he puts his bridge hand down to break off, I can actually see it swelling. It's red, it's purple and it's swelling right there before my eyes. He won the game and that was enough for me. I said I had to go.

The most famous Mike Baker story was when he was playing someone once in the summertime. It was warm, the windows were open and he said: "If I miss this, I'll jump out of that window." He missed. He just hopped across all the tables, got to the ledge and jumped out. The boys ran downstairs but he'd gone. It would only have been 12 feet or so, but it still wouldn't do the old legs or back much good.

All this was around 1967 when I knew I couldn't beat the real good guys downtown. I would walk about seven or eight miles in a day, calling in at 35 pool rooms. I'd make $10 here, lose $5 there, go on to the next one and make $50. My last stop was Broadway Billiards and that was where Mike Baker was. He had a very big following and to the kids he was their hero.

I hitch-hiked across Canada several times. Once, it was so cold that my friend and I had to start a fire by the side of the road. Another time, it was so cold and it was snowing so hard that I got inside an abandoned Volkswagen which had broken windows. I was so tired, I fell asleep. I woke up about half an hour later and I had about half an inch of snow all over me. So now I'm wet through, but I was lucky because some chap stopped for me in the next couple of minutes or so.

I once got stuck in a place called Nipagon which is 90 miles east from Thunder Bay at the top of Lake Superior. I got there late at night so I went to the police station to ask for some help. I slept in a cell, which was quite nice. I left there in the morning and walked across this big bridge which has a thousand foot drop. This gets you on to the Trans Canada highway and there's a signpost which says Sioux Saint Marie 350 miles. There are three towns on the way. One's called Marathon and the second is White River, which is the coldest place in our country. They're very proud of this big thermometer outside the city. At times, it's been down to 60 below.

When you stand with your thumb up, you stand at the back of this sign. On the back of it are things written like: "Help, I've been here for three days", and there's some drawings of some bones and some skeletons. It took me three days to get out of that town. I'd stand for 16 hours every day and then I'd go back to the police station and they'd put me in the cell for the night. I was trying to get to Toronto, but it was so cold there was no traffic going through. After three days I did a most stupid thing and just started to walk, I got about ten miles out into the middle of nowhere and I got picked up.

I was once in a place called Cash Creek. I got a ride up to the main road about five miles. It's real cold and it's 80 miles to the next town. I'm jumping up and down to keep warm and this guy stops. I get in, the heater's on and I'm thinking how great this all is and in just a couple of minutes he stops. We'd been going about a mile and a half. I wondered what the hell was happening and he said: "Here we are. That's my farm there." Then he dropped me off in the middle of nowhere.

I made so many journeys I can't put them in any kind of order. I remember one I made with Jack Pfeffer from Toronto. We went down to Detroit and we went down to Windsor, Ontario, to a pool room called Gilly. Gilly had the shaved down cue balls which made them lighter than the other balls so it made them easier to screw back. So each time Jack and I went down there we'd take our own cue ball and just slip it in. About the fifth trip, we were having a chat with Gilly and he said: "You won't believe this. My customers are nuts. They bring me cue balls." We had won thousands in there. There was also one very good player down there named Bob Chokolofovsky, who broke all of us at one time or another playing on a five by ten.

Jack was a very good front man to have with you. He was a good player and very knowledgeable. We were coming back one day from Montreal to Toronto, 320 miles, and he asked me whether I knew anything about the nap, about how the cue ball reacted on it in certain situations and the effect it had on certain shots. By this time I'd made a 145 break but I realised I didn't know a thing about the nap. We drove on mile after mile talking about the nap until we ran out of gas in the middle of nowhere.

I had a friend in Vancouver called Ed Smith. One night we had to go to Abbotsford, which was about 50 miles, and we had 30 minutes. We got there with five minutes to spare. He was doing about 130 in his sports car. I had four centuries that night. Eric Connelly was also there and we got snowed in. There's nothing better than being with two of your pals who are complete snooker nuts and you're snowed in and can't go anywhere. That to me was heaven.

Another time I went up to Prince George, BC, with Ed, who at this time had a car called AMX. It would do about 160. The only problem was that there was no rubber at the base of the gear shift, just a big hole for the air to come through. It was about 35 below, we're doing about 80 miles an hour, it's getting decidedly cool and we've got another 500 miles to go.

Every hour or so we have to stop off and get warm, have a cup of tea and get back in the car. Also, because it's so cold, and we've had some tea, we have to stop for a pee every 15 or 30 minutes. It was so cold that eventually we had to stop and check into a hotel. Next morning, we went out and bought one of those catolinic heaters. I stuck it right between my legs on the front seat so the fumes from this are coming out and mixing with the air which is whistling up through the bottom of the car. We go about 20 miles and I have a headache like I've never had before. So we stop the car and just throw the heater away. My headache lasted two days.

Donny Reeves came out to Vancouver for a spell and we're talking here about a guy who had made three or four thousand century breaks. He was a very good player but even good players go broke sometimes and when he wanted to play a guy for $20 he didn't have any money. So Donny went up to a guy called Fast Eddie Morris and borrowed Eddie's last twenty. I'm there, too, and I had a bet on the game because it seems that there's no way we can lose our money.

So Donny takes his jacket off and sticks it over the top of this peanut machine. It's on a stand and completely full of peanuts. He starts to play but he's missing everything so it finally gets down to the black at the end. The black's on its spot and he's right behind it so at last we're sure, despite everything, that our money's safe. But if I didn't know it before, I knew it then, if there's enough pressure, you can miss anything. Anyway, Donny, this player whose made all those centuries, leaves the black in the jaws and we've lost our money.

"What the hell were you doing there?" we wanted to know.

"Well," says Donny, "I really feel bad but you won't believe what I was thinking about. When I was shooting the black, I was thinking: 'Suppose that somebody walked into the room and they wanted to buy some peanuts, right, but they wouldn't know that there were peanuts because my jacket, right, was sticking over the peanut machine'." That's about as far gone as you can go, I think.

I ran into Donny at the race track in 1976. We hadn't seen each other for seven years. He's really into cards and horses now and doesn't play snooker. We shook hands and he was really pleased to see me. I was pleased to see him. Just then the warning for the next race came over the P.A. and Donny had to rush off to place his bet. He never came back.

One of the great Vancouver characters was Frank the Hustler who was sometimes known as Suitcase Sam. There was also a Chinese guy called Oil Can Harry who never ever won at snooker and Frank put him through like you wouldn't believe. Frank started to play him for about $5 or $10 a game. Then they're up to $100, and then $500 a game and Frank's letting the guy beat him so badly that Frank has lost about $4,000 to him. The guy says to Frank: "Be here tomorrow at one o'clock because I'm going out tomorrow to sell my house."

This Harry wants Frank really bad. He goes out to the bank and draws twenty grand. Frank doesn't show up at one o'clock but the Chinese guy's there, 1.30 – two o'clock. This Harry is walking up and down the street outside the place with his cue in the rain. He's looking for this guy. Frank shows up a little after two and just beat the guy for everything he had.

The first time I ever saw Frank in Seymour Billiards in Vancouver he was wearing a tee shirt, the pants with the straps and had one track shoe and one wellie. There was a shoe shine place in the pool room and he went up to it and stuck out his wellie. This guy made fortunes. One of his big scams was that he would be up in the pool room and he would have another guy on the street trying to pick out a sucker. His friend would spot one and say: "Listen, how'd you like to make a buck?"

"Sure, what do I do?"

"Well, you see this pool room here. Well, I'm barred from it, but if you took this package up to my friend – my friend has the pink hat on . . ." Once that guy goes up the stairs he's gone because Frank could persuade anybody to play.

One day I asked one chap to play and he said: "Fine". But he wouldn't play for a dollar or even for the table. He said he just didn't gamble. I went off to have a coffee and when I came back five minutes later Frank the Hustler has this guy at the back of the room. The guy's got his wallet out and Frank has got the guy's wallet counting the guy's money.

THREE

GETTING SOMEWHERE

ONE OF MY FRIENDS in Vancouver, Randy Vaughn, told me about the action in San Francisco, particularly a game called pink ball they played in Cochrane's on a 12×6 snooker table with trap pockets – so called because they trapped any ball that wasn't going straight into them. The pockets were so small there was no way you could pot a ball down a cushion except just to roll it in at pocket weight and obviously you couldn't play a ball at that speed when you're playing for money.

The balls were racked up with the red at the apex, then the yellow and green with the pink in the middle of the back row with brown and blue either side. You had to shoot the balls in rotation and the game would normally be $5 a ball and $10 for the pink. It was also double for a run out. When you had 12 or 13 guys playing all at once it was possible to win about £700 if you broke and ran out. They wouldn't allow more than 12 or 13 guys in the game. When I started to play, the game had already been going on for two months. Some guys would play two or three days at a time, go home and sleep and come back in the game.

There were guys in the game like Philippine Gene, Joe Smiley, Hippy Dave and Nick the Greek, who was a card player and pool player from New York. He wore diamond rings and all that and he'd walk in with this beautiful doll and she'd sit there. And sit there. And then her make-up would start to run. And she'd sit there. She's beautiful when she comes in but by the time she leaves she looks just evil.

There was a guy we called Bullock. He was black and weighed about 200lb. He could light the room up with his teeth. He always used to bet on me. Every time I made a good shot he would smile and he'd say: "Come on C.C. Cut it C.C." C.C? Canadian Cliff.

Pretty well all these guys were taking bennies so they were, as we used to say, wired. Most of these guys had backers so they had to stay awake as well. There were normally six or seven guys waiting to get into the game. They might have been waiting a day, or two days, so they're popping pills as well. So, one way and another, there's about 40 guys involved and they're all stoned on speed pills or whatever. Once a guy brought in about 2lb of marijuana and just sat there in the pool room sorting it into small bags.

At the end of each game all the players, or their backers, would stick the money down on the table, piles of it. I was the first guy to break and run out twice in a row. The break-off shot was just to hit the reds as hard as you could and hope for the best. To break and run out was like making two 130s back to back, the table was so tough. I broke and ran out once and made about $2,200 but sometimes you might go an hour without getting a shot. Then, when you've spent an hour just paying out all this dough and you do finally get a shot, it could be a tough one. I was the first person to be barred from the game. I'm kinda proud of that now, but at the time I thought: there goes my livelihood.

While I was playing in Cochrane's, I was getting better all the time and I was starting to get some backers. There was one guy, whose name was Roy Bell. He was a mulatto. He always wore a hat and always carried a gun. I was so naive I thought that being with a guy who had a gun was quite safe.

He said to me one day that I was going to play Skinner the Bus Driver across the bridge in Oakland. We parked the car and to get into this place we had to walk along a corridor which was about 50ft long. It looked a little nasty in there. There was one light bulb for the whole place apart from the lights over the table. This Roy made the game and I was so much better than Skinner that I was soon up $600 or $700. Then I noticed a chap watching me who was a friend of Skinner's. He had a gold chain. The chain was off his neck and he was swinging it. He said: "There ain't no white boy ever gotten out of this place with Skinner's money."

But my backer had a gun so I just kept on playing. I was so dumb. I won one more game and I looked over and the fellow was smiling at me. Sixty five square feet of teeth in a black face. He pulled his jacket aside so I could see a gun in a holster. I thought: "He's got a gun. Roy's got a gun. That's one all." There's Roy and me, a stringbean, and there's about six of them.

Roy came over to me and said: "Cliff, I'm sorry to have to say this but I think you're going to have to lose back all the money that we've won".

I said: "No way".

He said: "Look, you've got to do that. Plus, to be on the safe side, you should dump some of our money."

So I just stopped trying, not making it too obvious. We got out in one piece but it could have been fairly serious if Roy or myself had started to mouth off at them. It was good that Roy knew the score. Without him I'd have been in a lot of trouble.

Another of my backers were George Fraley, who was with me when I flew down to play a character called Fat Bill in Phoenix, Arizona, where they play snooker on a table with trap pockets. George used to sleep walk and I often used to wake up when we were sharing a room to find George crawling round, barking like a dog. Once, I heard the door close as George went out in the middle of the night. I grabbed the door and saw George going into the lift, completely naked except that he had his tie and hat on. I got to him at the front door of the hotel and shouted: "George, for God's sake."

"Jesus Christ, what the hell am I doing?" he said. We walked back upstairs and the next morning George didn't remember a thing.

Anyway, George and I flew down to Phoenix to play Fat Bill who was so big he made Bill Werbeniuk look like Cinderella. His mother gave him about $35,000 to $40,000 a year to gamble with. I remember once I potted the blue and left the cue ball on the blue spot. Bill wanted the blue to go on the spot so he just moved the cue ball slightly.

George said: "You moved the ball, Bill".

"You ain't in this mother-fucking game. You ain't in this mother-fucking game. You keep your goddam mouth shut," says Fat Bill. All this came out as if it was one word.

Just to make sure I got the point he came over to me and said: "You keep your mouth shut, boy". I had never opened it.

I missed the last black one game and I swept the chalk off the table. It exploded into fragments on the wall and Bill said: "Goddam it, if I'd smashed the mother-fucking chalk every time I missed the mother-fucking black there wouldn't be a mother-fucking piece of chalk left in mother-fucking Phoenix." Again, this came out all as one word.

A couple of years later I pulled into Phoenix again and there's Werbeniuk playing a character called Ronnie Allen. So I go straight back out of the door and just peek in through the window. I get somebody to go in and say that I was in town and at such and such a hotel. Bill loses some money and he and his backers come back to the hotel. His backers now say they would like to back me. I remember one of these guys carried a gun and in fact he shot someone about two years later. I think he's still in jail right now.

Bill said that Ronnie Allen knew what I looked like and so we decided I should shave off my moustache and wear my hair in a pony tail. I probably cut myself in about 15 different places doing this. So I play Ronnie Allen and I have to give him some money on the odds, like 275–200. The first game, he broke and ran out so now I'm down 550 which means I've got to knock the balls in four games in a row to get ahead because to break and run out at pink ball is double.

Now, all of a sudden, I can't play and he beats me for 3,000. I've put myself through all this and all I've done is to lose Bill's backers their money. There was a mirror there and in the last game that we played I just happened to turn and look at myself. Looking at all these red blotches where I'd shaved and my pony tail, I just burst out laughing. To top it all off, some guys were passing round a billiard magazine from the States which had got my picture in it because by then I'd won some snooker tournament in Canada. These guys were saying: "That's him, sure, that's him," and all that so in the end I just turned round and yelled: "Yeah, that's me. So fucking what?"

So now it's war and now I phone up my friend Randy Lee from Victoria BC. He flies down next day with some more money. Next day, we play $250 a game and I lost two thousand. Randy flew home again that night.

Ronnie Allen is something else, a great player and a very good conman. He could play with one hand and just the shaft of a two-piece cue and he could run out at nine ball, just like that. The shaft was 19oz but even so . . .

My other big attempt to be a master of disguise was also a failure in the end. I would sometimes go by the name of Joey Johnson from Seattle, Washington. I'd go into town in this old mechanic's uniform, which was absolutely filthy, and stop by a gas station and stick some grease all over my hands. I'd remember the name of a gas station so I could say I worked there, and go into town to a pool room.

In Odessa, Texas, once I beat a guy for about $700 and he says to me: "Where you from, boy?"

"Seattle, Washington."

"You working round here?"

"Yeah."

"Where?"

"At the Mobil station down the road."

"Yeah, which one?"

I said such and such on such and such a highway.

He said: "No you don't."

I said: "Sure I do."

He said: "No you don't, I own the place."

The guy was very good about it. In some bad town, I would have been gone like in *The Hustler* where they broke Paul Newman's thumbs. Every time I see that scene or somebody mentions it, I remember the crack as his thumbs broke.

Actually, I have to say that I found the psychology of *The Hustler* and *The Color of Money* spot on. I loved the scene in *Color of Money* where the guy asks Tom Cruise what he's got in his case and he says: "Doom".

One character I played in San Francisco was known as Canadian Dick. I once won $1,000 dollars off him at $30 a game. It took 54 hours non-stop. He came in with a jar of speed pills to stay awake, but I really knew he had come to play when he flipped his cue case open and laid out three pairs of socks.

I played another guy, Bill Medlum, for $30 a game and after 30 hours I had him down to his last barrel. This gave him an edge because then I knew I could only win another $30. I won that and he pulled a gun out of his pocket. It looked like he had his finger through the trigger. He walked towards me and I thought I was going to die. He passed me and I thought he was going to shoot me in the back. When I turned round, he was selling the gun for another $30. He won six or seven games off the bat after that. I took a long time to get it back. Bill played on diet pills and called for a Bromo Seltzer every 30 minutes. I beat a guy named Herman the German for some money in Oklahoma City.

Joe Smiley and Hippy Dave said that Juarez, Mexico, just across the border from El Paso, Texas, was a great place for action. So we went down there. You can see in five seconds that this pool room was a real bad place. There was only one light bulb in the whole joint but what really put me off was that there was this picture on the wall and this guy throwing a knife into it. The picture was of the President of the United States. So we went right back down the stairs.

We were stuck for something to do so that's how we ended up in a brothel, the only one I've been in. Joe and Dave each went off to a room and this nurse examined my equipment and sent me upstairs, too. Whether it was the money, the surroundings or a bit of the puritan in me, I just knew that there was no way. I sat on the bed talking to this girl for about half an hour and met up with Joe and Dave outside. They seemed pretty happy and they asked me how I'd made out.

"Great," I said.

I had made one previous trip to San Francisco. I'd been down there quite briefly with Tom Cawley shortly after a disastrous trip on the ferry to Seattle with about $30 or $40 between us. The ferry was $5 each and after a few games of snooker and pool we were broke. We had to borrow $6 each off the Canadian government to get home and we made a pact that I was going to be the world snooker champion – despite not having any idea how to go about even entering it – and that Tom was going to be the best poker player in the world. He did, in fact, play in the world poker championships in Las Vegas, although he didn't win it.

We had taken the ferry from Victoria to Port Angelus, which is about 16 miles across the strait of Juan de Fuca. The idea was to drive down to San Francisco in his Volkswagen. We'd been planning the trip about a month. Tom got into a card game and he was sure that he had just been bluffed out of a pot. So now it's the last hand and Tom has all our trip money there on the table. I'm watching with very sweaty hands. I can't wait to travel 36 hours in a Volkswagen. The hand ends up with Tom and this same fella again and it ends with Tom putting all our money right in the middle. I'm praying the guy will call so we'll have this big stack of money but instead he folds. Tom flips his cards over and he has absolutely nothing!

Tom is a good guy but somehow he was always a jinx on me. I just never seemed to win when he was around. He was my backer when we went down to San Francisco that first time. He had about $900 on him and I had about ten. Pretty much as soon as we got there we headed for the race track at Bay Meadows. I bet $2 on this horse, the race starts, and as the horses come towards me I'm shouting my horse on. Tom comes up besides me and starts to shout for another horse. My horse just wins it by a nose and I'm jumping up and down, I'm so happy. I've won $12. He just looked at me and said: "We're broke." Tom had bet the $900 all on this race.

Another place in San Francisco is Palace Billiards, which is a beautiful room with mirrors all round it. They had very good tables, which is why the players liked it, although there were a lot of bad people roaming about. I was down and out for a while and slept in there for about a month. There would be four or five of us who would just go to sleep on a bench at night. I'd just keep my toothbrush in my pocket. San Francisco also had what was at the time the worst hotel in the world. It was called the Gordon Hotel. It was $1.50 each night, to be paid at noon, and the filth of the place was indescribable. But for a while I couldn't even afford that.

Palace Billiards was wrecked one day. Fortunately, I missed it. It was the headquarters of the Filipinos, but on this afternoon a motor-cycle gang came in drunk and started shouting abuse at them. The Filipinos threw them down the stairs, but they came back later with 30 or 40 more friends. They had guns and just wrecked the joint. All the mirrors were smashed. My friend Randy Vaughn dived over the bar counter and hid on one of the shelves underneath. Eventually, the Filipinos drove them back down the stairs by throwing snooker and pool balls. There must have been six racks of balls lying in Market Street outside the palace that day. I decided it was time to leave town.

In 1968 I played my first supposedly official competitive match. There were four entries for the Canadian professional championship and I lost to Don Maybee. I made 45 first shot, but by that time I couldn't breathe any more so I missed more or less on purpose. The same trip, I won the Toronto city championship. I beat Winnie McKinley in the final and the first prize was $200.

It might have been on that trip to Toronto that someone said to me, quite casually, that Mo La Plante had been killed in a car crash in Sudbury. He was the first person I knew really well that was killed or had died. He was as close to me as anyone I've ever met. You think a bit differently after a thing like that. You think (a) life's not so bad and (b) it doesn't go on for ever.

On 20 July 1969, when Neil Armstrong took his first steps on the moon, I was picking cotton in Deli, Ontario. The temperature was about a hundred. My job was to walk in front of the horse. The horse's name was Nell. The cotton pickers sat on the machine which Nell pulled. It was a horrible job. You really had to need the money to even consider doing it. It paid $1.50 an hour. Finally, what with the boredom and the heat and the sheer drudgery, I came to a halt and Nell ran right into the back of me, slobbering down my back. It was time to quit but the trouble was that it wasn't as easy as all that.

The farmer was a fierce man, for ever going on and on about boys whose spines were made of jelly. One night, a hobo was holed up in his barn so he just took his shotgun and blazed away at the barn like a madman.

The night after Nell ran into the back of me I went downtown to a pool room and won about $300 playing on a table with a red cloth. We played with 15 yellows instead of 15 reds. There was no way I was going to work another day. I got in around two in the morning and everyone had to be up at five to start work. Straightaway I went looking for the farmer to tell him I was quitting. He was pulling a cart loaded with hay. The cart was maybe 15 feet long and piled high. He'd attached himself to the lead that normally goes round the horse and he was just pulling it by his own strength.

As it was obvious he could kill someone with his bare hands, I was nervous. "Er . . . ah . . . Er Mr so and so. I have to quit." I said. That was all I did say because as soon as he heard this he let go of the cart with a heave that sent it right over on its side and started coming towards me.

I just ran. I ran all the way into town, which was about six miles and for about the first two miles he was right behind me. I was never paid for the hours I'd worked, but I was just glad to shake him off. I learnt my lesson from this. I never worked again.

A couple of months later, I heard from my Uncle Bill in Vancouver that my Aunt Marge was trying to get hold of me. She said my mother wanted to see me. This was a big surprise because the whole family had been telling me for 20 years that she was dead. When she left, my mother had apparently left me tied up in a chair so my dad would find me when he came home from work.

Anyway, I knocked on my mum's door and when she opens it I say: "Hello mum, it's me, Cliff".

And she says: "Kip". She said she used to call me that.

She had four children then by her second marriage and the children were aged about 17, 10, nine and six. I stayed there that night. Up to then I'd only heard one side of the story so this was my first opportunity to hear her side of it. As always, there seemed to be some faults on both sides. Now, I think that she was more at fault than my dad, but as I wasn't there all the time, or at least couldn't remember it, how can anyone tell for sure?

For about the next ten years I used to spend a week or two with my mum in Vancouver every summer. Then we had a disagreement and she sent me back the tapes of all my matches. When she did that I felt as if she'd done again what she'd done to me when I was a baby. This really bothered me for about a month or so, but now I just don't care about it any more. I'm here, she's there, that's fine with me.

I found the whole experience of meeting my mother after thinking she was dead all those years very disorientating. The more I thought about it, the more upset I was that my family hadn't told me the truth, instead of just pretending that she didn't exist any more. It made me look at my dad, my aunts and uncles a bit differently. I couldn't believe that they could treat me as some kind of dimwit and not tell me, not treat me like an adult. Maybe that's how they treated my father as well.

The biggest effect it had on me, I guess, was to make me try even harder to make something of myself. Now, when I think of it, I know what they've done but I still can't see why they did it. It seems to me that it was they that had the problems.

In November 1969, I won the Western Canadian championship in Calgary. I'd been playing three and a half years and for the first couple of years I'd played mainly pool. I played some snooker but I hadn't been into snooker long enough to understand its patterns. I didn't have this problem with pool and, number one, I had to make a living.

I beat Bill Werbeniuk in the final of the Western Canadian 4–2. Up till then Bill and I had always been barred because we played for money, but a guy called Bob Kelly, who was a hockey player, organised it so that Bill and I could play. Bob had lived in Scotland in the early Sixties and had got to know John Pulman, so when he came home about 1965 he started promoting snooker.

Occasionally we saw snooker magazines from England and we just couldn't understand how John Spencer had beaten Rex Williams 55–18 in the 1969 world semi-finals. None of us even considered the possibility in those days that all the dead frames were played out. John and Rex's match had been best of 73, played over a week, so we just wouldn't have been able to take in that once John had got 37 frames, which he would have done about the Thursday night, that they just went on playing right up to Saturday evening.

What was really exciting about the Western Canadian was that people had actually paid admission to watch. This was something absolutely new to Bill and myself and a few of us just started to discuss the possibility that we were part of something people wanted to see.

Then two good friends of mine in Toronto, Wayne Kimura and Dennis Hahn, decided to bring over Rex Williams and Fred Davis in November 1970. I remember that George Chenier died about that time.

Bill and I had to go from Vancouver to Toronto by train. The whole way across I practised by cueing into a bottle and Bill, for some reason, was playing with the rest all the time. Bill also ended up giving a guy a snooker lesson for $5. This was on the train with no table and no balls.

When we got to Toronto, Bill beat me 4–2 and he played Thornley. Then Thornley beat Bill 4–2 mostly on experience because both Bill and I were playing a lot better than Paul by then, and then Fred beat Rex 4–2. Fred played a shot in the final against Paul that has always stood out in my mind. He powered the black in just off straight, so that the cue ball just missed the jaws. It floated just by the pink on its spot and got right on the red by the cushion in the only place the red would go. I had never seen a shot like that before in my life.

Fred beat Paul 4–1 in the final. We played at the North York Centennial Centre which had about 2,000 capacity and we had crowds of more than 600.

Both Fred and Rex were very nice to me. I liked the way they played and the way they talked and I just couldn't believe the suits and the clean shirts. At that time, wherever I was when I woke up, I used to put on my least dirty shirt but I thought then and there that I wanted to be like them.

It's a shame that Rex hasn't been as successful as he should have been. Perhaps he started to think too much. Perhaps his thinking has been a little negative. It seems sometimes that he's thought too much about what he's got to lose. It's always struck me as a little funny that he hasn't played in the billiards championship for the past few years, even though he's obviously either the best player or at least one of the best players. What's the point in being a good player if you don't compete?

I have to say, though, that I've had some great times with Rex. He's got very involved with the politics of the game, but away from all that he can be great fun. When the players are away in strange places, they sometimes get bored and they only have each other's company to rely on. One of the low points for boredom was years later in New Zealand when Rex and I were both so desperate that we ended up going to see Captain Nemo at a children's matinee.

Meanwhile, Fred and Rex went home and I was asked to become resident professional at a place called The House of Champions which was kept by Steve Turay in Toronto although Al Selinger bought it off him later on. He gave me $50 a week and I played about six or eight hours a day there for most of the summer of 1970. I used to set off each morning carrying a little lunch bag and take the bus just like anyone else going to work. The theory was that I would attract a few people down to the room but I don't think it worked out as well for Steve's business as it did for my game.

I made my first 147 there. I lost count of the times I took 12 or 13 blacks and then finished somewhere around the yellow with some impossible shot to hold position for the next black, but I finally made two in a month. When I'd made ten, I checked back and found that I'd also taken 15 reds, 15 blacks 43 times and then flubbed up on the colours. So why was it if I could usually run out the colours eight or nine times out of ten that I only did it one in four after I'd taken 15 reds, 15 blacks?

Then I got word that there was a guy in Billings, Montana, who was the state nine ball champion but who also liked to play snooker. I was a road player rather than a hustler. I very rarely went to any lengths to conceal my ability. I didn't always like to advertise who I was or where I was from, but I never played any guy for a sucker unless he was trying to do it to me.

I went there with Bill Werbeniuk. We parked the car a couple of blocks away because the Canadian number plates would have given it away that we are snooker players.

When I located this guy I found he wasn't much of a nine ball player. Soon I was way ahead of him. So then he decides he's going to win his money back at snooker.

"I don't want to play none of your snooky," I told him. My accent for the occasion was like something out of *Gone with the Wind*.

"You took all my money. Now we'll play for $100 at snooker," he yells.

"No, I don't feel like playing right now."

32

He went on and on and I eventually let him play for $200 a game. He gave me nine points a frame start. He couldn't play snooker at all and I took nearly all his money.

So now this guy was desperate. He challenged Bill, who he thought was just my backer not knowing that Bill was a better nine ball player than I was. Bill took what little he had left. Bill's nickname at the time was The Garbage Collector.

When I went on the road with Bill we took with us Kurt Berrow, who'd been in the top ten heavyweights in the world about five years previously. Kurt was fantastic protection and in strange towns you needed it, so the deal was that he would get a third of anything we won. The trouble was that if we won, say, $600, he'd go right out and spend his $200 on clothes. So if we lost and went broke Bill and I had to pay it all ourselves. This made Bill very angry.

I once played a character called Stockton Billy in Stockton, California. Kurt was there and Bill had been drinking very heavily. It's very rare that you see drink have much effect on Bill but this time he made some comment to the guy who was backing Stockton Billy, something to the effect that the guy had no guts or no class.

I was up about $400 and we were playing $50 a game. I was just going along quite nicely and here is Bill getting these guys going. Suddenly I'm playing a game for $200 which I didn't want to do because of my inexperience of playing nine ball. So then the guy that's backing Stockton Billy grabs the $200 when he beats me and sticks it in Billy's pocket. Then he turned to Bill and said: "*That's* class." Then the owner of the place started to get into a beef with Bill. This guy was pissed out of his brains. Bill said something, the guy said something and then the guy said: "I'll be right back".

Two minutes later, all the lights in the place go out. The money is stuck in one of the pockets on the table and I'm there, at the most, in two seconds but it was gone. Now we hear this big bang. The lights are still and out and I'm saying: "Kurt, Kurt . . ." and Bill's screaming for him too. Kurt goes to the door and opens it so that we can see and then the lights come on. Then we go out the front and there's this owner passed out on the floor and he has a gun in his hand. I think he must have turned the lights out and banged his head on something. With things like that, I started to become a bit disillusioned with the whole scene.

I went back to Vancouver and married my first wife, Susan Byatt, who, I have to say, is still the best dancer I've ever seen in my life. Everything happened very quickly and it lasted about a year and a half. She had a daughter from before and we stayed at her mother's place. I was playing snooker all the time. I was totally obsessed with it. I was having a great time and I was getting better all the time. Finally, it came to the ultimatum: snooker or me. To this day, I still don't know if she thought she was giving me an 'out' in a classy way rather than just saying 'I don't love you' or something like that. I don't think she could have been that naive. I think she probably went out the classy way so as not to make me feel bad. Maybe it was the easy way out for both of us.

I won the Western Canadian again in the fall of 1971. The previous time we played best of seven. This time we played best of 73 and I beat Bill Werbeniuk 37–14. I made a 146 in a dead frame with a referee and a proper audience. Some people thought this beat George Chenier's 144 official Canadian record, but to me nothing can ever be a record unless it's made in a live match. The place where we played in Vancouver was named after him, Chenier Hall. It had a matchroom for about a hundred people. It was run by Glen Ferguson and John Forster and the game greatly needed this type of environment at the time. It was about an hour before play was due to start on the second evening that I met George Crum for the first time. George was then guest conductor for the opera *Il Travatore* but his main job was musical director of the Canadian National Ballet. He is definitely one of the leading men in that field. It seemed kind of out of place when he showed up, immaculately dressed and very quietly spoken, to ask if this was where the championship was taking place. I happened to be standing by the front door and George seemed to be amazed that he actually found himself talking to one of the players. There was a taxi there and George had come from downtown, which would have been about $20. So my first impression was that this guy must love the game. We had a drink afterwards and I actually went to the opera with my first wife two or three days later. The singing was great but it was in Italian and it wasn't really my type of scene. Ballet I can stand.

My next trip to Toronto I phoned George up and went to his place for dinner. He became good friends with Paul Thornley and he's become one of my best friends. He came with me once to a flat where I was living and we could hear someone learning to play the piano in one of the other flats. It turned out that it was a little girl. Her mother invited us in. George listened and was very nice to her and then asked if she would like him to play something for her.

George sat down and played something absolutely beautifully and just to see this little girl's eyes was beautiful. I guess this shows what sort of guy George is. He's one of the biggest snooker nuts that I've ever met, a very classy snooker groupie. He's made an 80 break but he's quite short and carries a lot of weight so his shape is against him being a really good player. When he retired from the musical director business he opened a snooker club and one or two people have pointed out to me how strange it is that the hands which conducted all those masterpieces over the years are now used for serving up hamburgers for his customers and things like that. But George is really happy in snooker so that's that.

When George Chenier died, a guy named Major Jim Farley Faulkner, who was about 65 and who had high jumped for Canada in the Olympics, decided to revive the North American championship. He had some foresight in wanting to make snooker bigger and his idea was to have a tournament in the west in Calgary and one in the east in Toronto, with the two champions meeting for the North American title. I won the west but then this idea was scrapped so the one in Toronto became the North American championship. Hardly anything was ever printed about snooker in Canada in those days, but I see that in January 1972, *Snooker Scene* reported that I beat Kenny Shea from Dartmouth, Nova Scotia, 36–15 at the House of Champions in the final. I made a 134 break and missed the pink. I would have had $1,100 bonus if I'd made a maximum.

My memory of the whole thing is pretty confused, but I can remember thumbing my way from Vancouver to play in the tournament in Toronto. I got a ride from a guy in Brandon, Manitoba, who was driving from Anchorage, Alaska, to New Jersey, about 6,000 miles. He had some kind of pills to stay awake and for some reason he was going to have to drive all the way back again about five days later. Not only did this guy give me a ride all the way. He also took me to the door and lent me $20.

The early part of the tournament was some kind of round robin. There were about 70 entries and we each had to play each other three frames. I forget just how long it took to play. I lost the title in the winter of 1972–3. Bill Werbeniuk had to play Eddie Agha to see who played me for the title. I can't remember a damn thing about the match, but I'll never forget Major Jim Farley Faulkner's introduction:

"Ladies and gentlemen . . . welcome to blah, blah, blah . . . in this corner . . . from out of the East . . . blah, blah, blah . . . Atomic Eddie Agha. In this corner . . . from outta the West . . . Burly, Battling Bill Werbeniuk . . . and your referee, Bill Ti- Tanic." This really was the referee's name: Bill Titanic. And he was, about 20 stone of him. The only thing was, he kinda spoilt the effect by walking on with his thumbs in the loops of his belt hitching up his trousers over his enormous gut. Bill beat me 25– 21 in the final.

Eddie Agha was the best player in Montreal in the Sixties. He made two 147s and he was pretty good once he was in the balls but he was too short to be a really complete player. He was also born about 15 or 20 years too soon because when he was playing well there was nothing for him to play in. I remember Tony Knowles once underestimated him very badly in the Canadian Open in the late-Seventies and Eddie knocked him off about 9–2.

Tony Le May was another French Canadian although he's been in Toronto for years and has made quite a name for himself as a coach. He's given me some help from time to time. His favourite line after he beats a guy for some money is: "Eh! I make you see the train go by".

Terry Haddock brought me back from Vancouver to be house professional in his club in Toronto for $3–400 a month. I made three 147s in eight days in one spell.

Tony Le May who is built like the The Whale, who I knew in Toronto, and Fat Bill from Phoenix, Arizona. Tony coaches at Le Spot in Toronto

That was when I stopped keeping track of my centuries. By then I was making about 50 a month and I'd got up to 600 so I stopped counting.

I saw Kirk Stevens there for the first time in the summer of 1972. People were queueing up to play me at a dollar or two a game. All of a sudden this young kid comes along. He was 12 and so short for his age that he had almost a side-arm type of action. He asked if he could play me and then he said he would like to play for $2 the same as everybody else. I offered him 70 start, but he said he would like to play level. So I beat him two games and he paid me the $4. I'd never seen money like it in my life. It was like it had been in his pocket for six years and his pants had been washed about 50 times. I said to him that he probably needed the money more than me but he said: "No, here you are. You've earned it."

The next time I played him was in the 1978 Canadian championship. I beat him 6–1, but then he beat me 7–5 in the semi-final in 1979. This was in the days when both amateurs and professionals played in it. I didn't see much of Kirk in those years because for most of the time he seemed to be with the wrong crowd. These guys were okay to have some fun with but not if you wanted to be a professional snooker player. I could see this, my friends could see it and the people who knew Kirk could see it, but what could you do? He had this horrible thing when his mother was killed in a fire which somebody had started on purpose and the whole world knows now that he developed a drug problem but I can't help thinking that Kirk should have grabbed hold of himself more than he did. We didn't get to know each other much until Kirk moved over to England in September, 1980.

Anyway, in that summer of 1972 I'm quite happy at Terry Haddock's place and maybe this is the time to say that Terry did a lot for the game in Canada. He had his own business interests supplying tables and equipment and keeping clubs so it was understandable that he was a little selfish in certain ways, but he certainly did as much as anybody could have done in the circumstances. A couple of years later he set up a tournament at the Canadian National Exhibition in Toronto each August which, for a few years, a lot of the British players would come to and he also set up a couple of TV shows.

In the absence of anyone else, he did the commentary with an all-round TV sports guy named Fergie Oliver. At the time I used to give Terry 95 start so his idea of what shot I was going to play often turned out to be not that accurate. He used to say things like: "It looks as if Cliff is just going to cinch this ball," or "I think Cliff is going to try to leave him on the beach" – which sounded more like a war movie than a snooker commentary. As he was sat right beside the table I could hear every word he was saying. Once he said: "I'm sure that Cliff is going to shoot the blue," so I shot the brown on purpose.

Al and Betty Selinger, of Dufferin Cue, also did a lot for the game. They also made a great cue. I won the championship with one of theirs. When I first went to their factory, I realised that they were also very big in wooden toilet seats. There were thousands of them. Mike Holubik was another good guy who supported the game, although I have to say honestly I didn't like the tables he made. Doug McDonald, with guys like Gerry Seed and Erwin Budge in Ottawa, ran the Canadian championship in the Seventies, which was then for amateurs and professionals. I won it from 1974 to 1978 and then Kirk beat me 7–5 in the semi-finals in 1979. When I won it in 1977 it meant I could keep the trophy outright. I thought Doug's sense of showmanship was a little bit lacking when he presented me with the trophy out in the parking lot, but he did get Canadian participation in the world amateur championships organised from 1976 and he was instrumental in bringing the championship to Calgary in 1980.

When I won the North American championship in December 1971, I went back to Vancouver on the train with my first wife. John Spencer was doing an exhibition in Calgary. We stopped off there to see John's show and trick shots in this place called Billiard Square, which had 42 tables. The guy who owned it was called Phil Dephilipi. He blew his head off with a gun about 1985 so obviously something went wrong with his life, but at that time he was very keen to get something going in snooker. He put up the idea to some other guys that John and I should play some matches, starting off right there in Calgary, going up to Edmonton and then down to Vancouver, which was then my home town, so to speak.

They liked the idea so John came back in March after he'd lost to Higgins in the 1972 world final and I played him two sessions a day for six days in Calgary, travelled a day, did the same in Edmonton, travelled another day and ended up in Vancouver.

John beat me 56–49 in Calgary, which wasn't as close as it sounds because I won six of the last eight. John had 13 centuries and I had eight. There was seating for about 800 but with the scaffolding it looked pretty bare so Phil went out and bought 800 red cushions. After a day or two John had started to pull away so this one afternoon there were only about 30 people watching and all you could see was the wasteland of red cushions. Considering John had been world champion twice at that time, I felt pretty good about the match as a whole so I asked him if he thought I was good enough to be a professional in the sense of travelling over to England. He said: "Yes."

"How do I get into the association?"

"I'll put your name forward."

On the last night, I made five centuries in eight frames including three on the trot. Like an idiot, I asked John if he could see anything that was wrong with my game. He said: "I don't like the way that you twist your wrist." I couldn't sleep the whole night because of what he had said about twisting my wrist and I couldn't play properly after that for about a month.

John beat me 54–43 in Edmonton. I made a 144, which did tie George's record, and which was the biggest thrill of my life up to then. It put me in line for the high run prize which was $250 but John made a 147 in the last session.

The next week we had a press conference in the Georgia Hotel, Vancouver. Phil was a nervous type of guy and the strain was really getting to him by now. I phoned him up in his room and he said: "Good afternoon, Billiard Square". This was the place he ran in Calgary, 600 miles away. Phil had set up this 10×5 table in the lobby and John and I were going to do this little show on it to drum up some interest for the match. Then Phil discovers that he hasn't brought a triangle to rack the reds. So there he is trying to rack the balls with his hands and his arms and he has about two inches of ash on his cigar. There are about 200 people standing around. He just gets the balls racked and all of a sudden the ash goes right in the middle of the balls. So then Phil is starting to blow and smooth the ash away and just trying to pretend this hasn't happened. The balls all start to drift down towards the blue spot and of course he has to start again.

John beat me 42–33 in Vancouver, in the Exhibition Gardens which holds about 1,200 people. The score sounds quite respectable but, in fact, John slowly demolished me. I learned a lot from playing him, but I was really fed up by the end because I knew he was a much better player than me.

One of the farcical things about those three matches was that I played in the only suit that I owned. We were playing two sessions a day so there never seemed to be time to have it cleaned or go out and buy one. And because I didn't like flying I had to drive on the rest days as well.

Anyway, through meeting John, I had actually come to grasp the mechanics of how to become a proper professional, how to enter the world championship and how to get to England. He proposed me as a member of the professional association and I entered the next world championship that was held in April 1973.

FOUR

GOING LEGIT

I DIDN'T like flying. I still don't. At the airport I had about six or seven drinks because I was trying to figure out how my obituary would read in the paper if the plane went down. I thought it probably wouldn't be that big because I hadn't done anything. I was so happy when the plane landed safely.

I was with Berit Christiansen, who I'd met on the rebound after my first marriage broke up about six months previously. When we landed in London the first thing I noticed was that the air was fresh, thick and damp. It was very strange. We stayed at the Cumberland Hotel. West and Nally, who were running the championship, had their offices just round the corner in Berkeley Square. I met Simon Weaver for the first time and a fellow named Jacob de Vries.

Higgins was in town at the time and somehow he asked me if I wanted to play snooker for a fiver a game. He said that he'd give me 40 start. Being the gentleman that I am, I only took 28. I don't think he won a game. All I remember is Higgins at the top of some stairs, I'm running down the stairs, I still haven't been paid, and he's got a ball in his hand, threatening to throw it at me.

That was the first time I'd met him. We just never really got along since that moment.

David Greaves and his wife, Christine, opened their doors to us in Blackpool. When I went up there, David fixed six or seven shows for me at about £10 a time. At the time I was getting £50 a night back home, but as I obviously played better at home, I was certainly better value at £50 in Canada than £10 over here.

I really struggled. My hands felt clammy all the time, the balls felt very, very heavy. I think this was the first year that Super Crystalates were used. They were lighter than the Crystalates which had been used in Britain before but they felt very heavy compared with the Vitalite I was used to in Canada.

This is how I looked on my first visit to England in 1973. I'm just about to break off in the plate final against John Pulman with a man and a dog watching. Actually, I'm not too sure about the dog

I didn't know very much about the naps of cloths until I came over here. A half-ball yellow to roll it in and come back for the green off one cushion was a trial because I didn't know where to aim. Any shot like that I was hitting too thin and I just had no control at all. It took me at least three years to know that I'm not supposed to roll that yellow in but that on certain shots I should go to the side cushion and the other cushion and out. I lost so many games trying to roll the yellow slow.

So I had problems with the balls, the cloth and, of course, the size of the pockets. I just couldn't believe some of the balls that I missed, but in fact they were difficult shots. I thought I really didn't like the style of game over here. I didn't think it was conducive to my style of play.

Anyway, I had these six or seven shows with David Greaves. He had fixed about five of them through a guy called Mike Walker up in Keswick who has been a very good friend to me. I've been back to Keswick just about every year since then and Mike's daughter, Helen, who was only five when I first met him, is now our nanny for Jamie and Andrew. I like it up there. There's no speed, it's all very laid back and I like to play dominoes and drink some bitter by the fireplace when it's cold outside. I actually tell Mike that the only reason I go back there is that his wife, Pat, makes the best mince pies you can imagine. It was great for me that first time to know that we'd go back to Mike's place and have mince pies, two pieces of Pat's chocolate cake and some cheese.

Mike also took Bill Werbeniuk up to Keswick in 1974. He picked Bill up at the station and as they're driving along they see all these sheep rolling about. Bill asks Mike if he's got a gun, thinking they were wild and that it would be OK to shoot a couple and eat for dinner.

My last show was at Fleetwood and the next week I was playing Dennis Taylor in the first round of the championship. Dennis came over to watch and he since told me that he felt sorry for me because I was playing so badly and I was getting so frustrated.

Then I played Dennis at the City Halls in Manchester and I won 9–8. I was winning 8–6 and then it went to 8–8. In the last game, Dennis needed a snooker. I missed it and the whole place erupted. Apparently, there was a busload from Blackburn supporting Dennis. They were standing and shouting, stamping their feet. I really felt he was playing at home. I looked over and there was Terry Haddock, Rick Horgan and Berit from Canada, sitting there in the front row like lost sheep.

I didn't know what to expect in Britain but I used to joke around with my friend Wayne Simpson about what it would be like. We thought maybe the MC would be wearing a Beefeater's uniform and yelling: "Hear ye, hear ye!" In more ways than not, it was a lot better than I thought it would be. I felt very excited. That particular championship was the first to be all under one roof and there was a lot of tension. For all the snooker nuts, it was absolute heaven. I was very pleased with the way I played against Dennis. I hadn't played that well in practice. I just automatically played half-decent when the championship started.

Snooker Scene, under the headline 'Cliffhanger', reported the match as follows:

Cliff Thorburn 9 Dennis Taylor 8

Scores: 37–84, 76–36, 77–30, 52–66, 11–78, 38–98, 64–39, 62–52, 39–76, 79–36, 10–103, 71–44, 73–23, 62–61, 37–74, 15–75, 58–42. Highest breaks: Thorburn: 40. Taylor: 47, 61.

The Cliff Thorburn – Dennis Taylor match in the Park Drive world professional championship ended in incredible fashion with 700 spectators crammed round the No. 1 table for the tense final frame in which Taylor, needed a snooker on the pink and black, got it only to see Thorburn cut a thin pink into the middle pocket for the match.

Trailing 2–4 but level at 4–4 at the interval, Thorburn went into an 8–6 lead only for Taylor to get back in the match with a 61 break, the highest of the match, in levelling at 8–8 before the dramatic finale.

Taylor, who had made a 47 break in the first frame, looked from this fluent break and Thorburn's hesitant start as if he would win comfortably but the Canadian proved to have plenty of iron in his soul in putting bad shots and bad running to the back of his mind in his intense concentration on each shot.

Thorburn said afterwards: "It was like a bear pit out there, but it was great. I'm glad to have won because it would have been such a let-down to come so far and lose in the first round. I find the conditions very strange. I'm having to think what I do because the balls are heavier and the pockets are tighter. In Canada, I don't have to think. I just play automatically."

Against Rex Williams in the second round, I started feeling more confident. I felt I'd learned something. I realised there was still hope for me because I had been really down in the dumps. It crossed my mind that if I could win I would play John Spencer in the next round. I didn't think I could beat him at the time but I wasn't too worried about that. It was 11–11 going into the final session and I guess I could have won with more experience but at that particular stage of my development it all got a bit much for me. It went all the way to 15–15 and in the last frame I was 24 behind with only the blue, pink and black left.

Rex also wasn't thinking that clearly because when I snookered him, he missed the escape and hit the pink. It wouldn't have mattered if he'd only given five away but with the six it meant I could draw. I didn't like the shot he left me but I daren't let him shoot the blue, even though it was difficult, because it was game shot if he potted it. A couple of shots later, I left him with the blue and he potted it.

Again, *Snooker Scene's* report of the four sessions captured the drama of the match, in particular the decisive last frame.

Rex Williams 16 Cliff Thorburn 15

Scores: 46–35, 9–69, 65–55, 20–76, 59–78, 67–8, 84–9, 10–78, 67–47, 27–82, 69–36, 77–67, 40–71, 9–87, 22–64, 9–86, 61–54, 36–76, 63–48, 65–48, 72–41, 50–58, 76–56, 80–6, 90–16, 22–73, 57–71, 36–67, 29–60, 88–8, 76–47.

Thorburn and Williams treated each other with enormous respect in a tension-laden match in which Thorburn took the last three frames of the first day to lead 8–7. Thorburn made a competent 63 to win the third frame and looked slightly the more dangerous when he was in. Williams, lacking in confidence it seemed, could well have acquired some had he capitalised on a hard-earned 7–5 lead (after Thorburn had taken the last two reds and all the colours up to the pink only to miss an easy black for 6–6) but the Canadian proved that he does not crack easily by taking the remaining three frames.

The second day produced two marathon sessions and an unbelievable climax with the smallest match room jammed solid and ladders being miraculously produced from some forgotten corner of the building so that faces kept appearing over the top of the boarding some 20 feet up. The interval brought up 11–11, but Williams made a push for home by winning the first three at night to lead 14–11. Thorburn, who seems to blink only about once every five minutes, continued to apply unwavering concentration, however, and won the first four to go one in front with two to go.

Thorburn had matched Williams's nagging safety, had looked much the better potter and seemed in much better possession of his nerve, but knowledge and experience proved to be Williams's most faithful allies. The consensus of spectator opinion was overwhelmingly in favour of a Thorburn victory for, from a distance, there seemed little fear that Williams would pot much, but in the next frame he got in twice when the reds had opened to compile breaks of 47 and 41 to take the match to the final frame.

In this, not one but both players cracked and some of the mistakes would have been remarkable in a local league match. Thorburn had the first chance and missed a black off the spot. Williams struck the front with a 45 and then missed black off the spot, screwing into the reds, but left nothing.

A little later, Thorburn missed another black off the spot only for Williams to miss an elementary almost straight red from about three feet by a good six inches. When Thorburn missed a far from difficult last red to give Williams another gift opening with most of the colours on their spots, a quick end looked inevitable, but somehow Williams snookered himself on the green.

By now, both men were in such a high state of nerves that the match seemed certain to be decided by easy shots and mistakes, but Williams suddenly produced a sizzling green into the baulk pocket and took the brown to lead by 24 with only the last three balls left. Thorburn then left an extraordinary snooker from which Williams not only failed to escape, but unthinkingly played the shot so much too hard that he hit the pink to leave the Canadian able to draw. Two shots later, Thorburn left the blue near the baulk pocket but the cue ball glued to the top cushion from which position Williams very creditably took blue and pink for the match.

The players were very fluent. Nobody stalled around. I guess it was because they'd played in more tournaments than me. I'd probably played in about six or seven in my life before I played in the world championship. I didn't know what a good referee was. With his white gloves, I automatically assumed the guy was a poofter. It was all so prim and proper, it was like something out of a book. It was all so neat.

The players were all very, very good, even the so-called bad ones. They always seemed to know what to do in any situation when they got in the balls, but I was struggling because I didn't know what was going to happen half the time. I didn't know how the cue ball would respond and I had trouble getting the cue ball back down the table. I didn't know what shots to go for. I didn't know what a 50–50 shot was. They all looked 15–85 to me.

But when they were in the balls, all the other players looked very confident. They knew how big the middle pockets were and they knew certain angles. I probably had too much respect for the middle pockets. They seemed awfully difficult to me so I just tried to leave myself playing into the black pockets all the time.

I was impressed with their play, but my biggest problem was myself. I just couldn't read the game right. I was staring straight at the table and nothing was happening. My mind was a blank but I knew I had to shoot, so I'd shoot. Thank God I'm past that stage. In fact now, if I've got a problem, I'll stay there until I can sort it out in my mind or, at least, I won't be rushed. I still shoot sometimes before I've found the answer because, with some shots, there isn't one!

Once I'm in the balls now I just get down and knock them in, but that used to take me the longest time. Maybe it was coming over here knowing that I wasn't making any other money outside what I make when I'm potting balls that put a lot of pressure on me. I just didn't want to make any mistakes and consequently my game was bogged down with thinking. It took a long time to finally accept to myself that I knew what I was doing. I got through, making a half-decent living from about 1977 onwards, without having the sharp attitude, the sharp thinking I found around 1983. This sharpness was more to do with how I ran my life than anything at the table instead of just taking each day as it came with no particular plan.

I didn't see much of the final between Reardon and Charlton. I was probably sick of snooker by then. I was also sick for John Spencer, who had lost 23–22 to Ray in the semi-final after being ahead 18–12. He and Ray were the two best players for most of the Seventies and Ray was the best from 1973–1978. I always wanted John to win because I knew him so well. When John lost the semi-final, I was devastated by it. I think Ray was the better tactician. John really didn't like to play safe that much; Ray loved it. Ray also knew when was the right time to stick his neck out.

Higgins was always a danger but he was just a bit behind Ray and John. He's very gifted. He had a knack and a gift for the game and he was the best natural potter I had seen until I saw Jimmy White. When I first knew him, he had the cue ball on a string, long shots, shots with side, he could do practically anything. He also has tremendous grit and his 69 run out in the 1982 world semi-final against

At Thames TV for Ray Reardon's This is Your Life. It was all my own hair. Also in the picture are Joyce Gardner, Graham Miles, John Spencer, Eddie Charlton (front), Alex Higgins, John Pulman and Jack Rea (back)

Jimmy, when Jimmy needed only one frame to win, was the best I've seen in my life. But he's run his life like a guy driving a car with one wheel in the sand.

Reardon won the title by beating Charlton 38–32 after losing the first session 7–0. It was still thought essential to play this large number of frames, spread over five days, in a world final. Television lighting for snooker was then very unsophisticated and when coverage began on the fourth evening it was soon apparent that Reardon could see much less well than Charlton. Three consecutive frames put Charlton ahead but two of the most dazzling floodlights were switched off at Reardon's insistence and he led 31–29 starting the last day's play.

It was the end of Higgins's first reign as world champion, annihilated 23–9 by Charlton in the semi-finals after he had beaten Fred Davis 16–14 in the quarters. During the latter, rain stopped play while the venerable roof of the City Exhibition Halls, Manchester, was mended. Reardon made an extraordinary recovery to beat Spencer in their semi-final 23–22 after trailing 12–19.

It was the first time the championship was held in an eight-table venue over a fortnight rather than spread through a series of venues over a whole season. Snooker Promotions, a West Nally subsidiary, obtained the sponsorship of Park Drive and took the financial gamble as promotors, thus ushering in a new era in the promotion of the game.

I went home but came back in November because I had an invitation to play in the Norwich Union Open, another West Nally promotion, at the Piccadilly Hotel, London. I beat Patsy Houlihan 4–0 and lost to Higgins 4–2 and I still remember one game where there was a red sitting over a corner pocket. The balls were all split and instead of just rolling an easy red in and bouncing off a side cushion, I elected to shoot one that was on the top cushion and missed it. It was the most stupid shot you've ever seen in your life. I never played that one again. I felt really good, I felt good enough to beat him, but to make a serious error of judgment like that showed how inexperienced I still was.

Later in the week I got involved in a card game with Higgins, Werbeniuk and a guy called Black Jack from Vancouver. Higgins went broke and asked me to lend him £50. I'm losing as well so I say okay if he gives me his ring. By then I knew him. He gave me his ring. He's with Cara, his first wife, so that night she comes down to my room and demands the ring off me. I said no, so Alex pretended to faint on the floor. I went to pick him up but I turned my back on him and the guy grabbed a bottle. I grabbed him and threw the bottle down. I got my left arm round him and just pounded his head until my hand got sore.

I was also invited to play in the 1974 series of Pot Black which was recorded in Birmingham between Christmas and New Year 1973. I had the flu. There was no heat in the hotel. I was nervous. I'd never played on British television. I'd been considered the best player in Canada for the previous three or four years and I didn't know a thing.

Until my last match, my highest break was 13. When I cleared the colours against Jackie Rea – which meant Graham Miles qualified instead of him – he just couldn't believe it because I'd played so badly. He was stunned. Graham, who that year was the reserve and only came in because Fred Davis was ill, went on to win it.

We all stayed at the Strathallan and Joe Davis was there. We talked about George Chenier and he said at first what a great player he was. Then we really talked.

George was dead by then so I figured that he'd say something nice about him and the matches they'd played, but he just chuckled and said: "I knocked his cock off". Imagine, if Joe was like that when George was dead, what could it have been like when he was playing him?

Joe had so many good qualities but he had to run the game all by himself so he had to have a strong arm. If he'd quit in 1935, the game would have gone downhill from there. When he quit from the world championship in 1946 that was actually the beginning of the end for snooker. The world championship wasn't worth a bean because everybody knew the best player wasn't in it and Joe was still going round doing exhibitions. I got to wondering why Joe would do something like that. I know that Joe wanted to retire undefeated but how important is that? If a person did that today, kept on playing competitively but wouldn't play in the championship, it would be ludicrous. I also remember Joe saying: "At one time, Fred was a better player than me but he didn't know it".

Joe just had to win. One night we'd started to play poker and I had this light blue woollen suit on. A friend of mine called Lew Myles had found out that I was going to play in the world championship and had made these four suits for me. They were quite snappy at the time.

One hand I had was four sixes or something like that. Joe had four threes. I beat him and he was very, very upset about it. He grabbed all the money in the pot, squeezed it into a ball and put it in my beer. Somebody got the money out and there we were trying to dry it with lighters and sticking it by the fireplace. The very next hand, I had four eights and Joe had four sixes. He was shocked. He reached over, grabbed my waistcoat and ripped it. All the buttons popped and he said: "How many eights have you got in there for Christ's sake?"

My cigarette burnt a big hole in my suit. I'd got no buttons on my waiscoat. All my money is soaked. This sounds terrible but this was just Joe.

Then, Spencer and Joe were in the final of another hand. Joe had something like three kings and two queens so Spencer picked up two of Joe's queens and put them in his own hand. So Joe grabbed all the money that was in the pot and stuck it in a pint glass. Then John said: "Joe, I was just kidding. Two of these queens are yours." Joe just took the money out of the glass and put his pint all over Spencer's suit. Then John spilt his drink over Joe's suit. His shock was incredible. Nobody was speaking now. Then Joe did something really classy. He just said: "You bastard. What are you having?"

I thought this was really terrific. I was very glad that I didn't play in the time that Joe was running the game but he was one of the nicest men that I ever met and he was so much fun. It's nice to know men like him who you can admire.

He gave me a big thrill in Bermuda in 1976. There is an international snooker league which has teams from the Eccentric Club, the New York Athletic Club and places like that and Joe came along as a guest. I did some trick shots on the final night. I set one up with just the cue ball and the black and I cue the black in one-handed. To see Joe standing up clapping like a fan was really something. I also love the old black and white film of him making his first century on television. He was very quick, very polished, very complete.

The rest of the season I stayed up in Bolton. I met Tony Knowles and I played three or four games with him at his father's club. Vince Laverty and John Spencer looked after me. They had to because I appeared on their doorsteps nearly every night. Vince got me into a flat, the kind of place where I'd put 5p in and get some heat.

I used to play some guys at the Bolton Snooker Centre. There was one guy, Henry, who was a window washer, who I'd give 14 start. I was low in confidence at the time and he used to beat me. I used to get so mad and tired. One day, he beat me for £8 or something and it was blood money. I felt like saying: "I'm not eating tonight because of you". They were very depressing times because I wasn't doing anything constructive. I was playing snooker but under probably the worst conditions that I could possibly play under. It wasn't really doing me any good.

West and Nally arranged an exhibition in Cardiff for me for £50 which was one of the very few engagements I had. There was a train strike so I got the bus from the bus station in Bolton. The journey was nine hours and the bus was jammed full of kids. I got to the hotel and had about a half hour nap and woke up with the worst headache I've had in my life. There were fumes coming out of the radiator. It smelt like some type of chemical being burnt. I got to this club and of course these guys can't wait for me to get there. They're arguing among themselves whether I'll make a century in the first frame or not. My highest break of the night was 42. By the time I had paid for the bus and my board and meals I guess I made about £3.50.

The best experience I remember from living in Bolton was going with Vince and John to the final of the Stockport Advertiser tournament which at the time was one of the biggest amateur events in the north of England. There were about 600 there. Jack Rea, who was one of the top players in the fifties before he more or less gave up competing to concentrate on exhibitions, always did his trick shots at the Stockport Advertiser final. It was the first time that I had seen his routine and the tears were just running down my cheeks. I don't think I've ever laughed more and I learned a few things too.

The 1974 world championship was at Belle Vue, Manchester, in April and I beat Allan McDonald. This was harrowing because when he got up to play his shot he had to lean on the table with his head down and holding his stomach. He had cancer and he was fulfilling his life's ambition of playing in the world championship. I didn't like it at all. Snooker is about the only sport where they would have let him play. But his dream came true. He played. He went home to Australia. He died a few weeks later.

Then I played Paddy Morgan, a very good player who hasn't really made the most of himself. He's very likeable and easy-going and one of the great characters of the game. He hardly ever competes now and I miss him. He's from Belfast but he went out to Australia and after a while got a resident professional job. I was with him at one tournament and it seemed like someone was looking for him in a pretty heavy way.

I said to him: "Paddy, I can't stand this. You'll have to go back to your room now." He said he didn't want anybody to know where he was. I said: "That's fine," but I didn't want him in my room.

In this match at Belle Vue we played on the main match table. I was ahead 3–1. After that frame, he took off his tie, which I thought was a bit strange. Then he took off his waistcoat. I wondered what was happening. Then, in the next frame, he missed the black off its spot and he drop-kicked his chalk right out of the arena. He should have been playing rugby for Ireland. The chalk went up about 40 or 50 rows right out of the joint.

Belle Vue, Manchester. The venue for the 1974 world championship. There were eight separate mini-arenas, some of them better than this one. The floor was so uneven in places that some of the shorter players sometimes caught their knuckles on the cushion rail as they played a shot. Fred Davis was told that this was not because the table was high but because the floor was low. We don't have this problem at the Crucible

So then I lost seven out of the next eight. I lost 8–4. What with the referees, the tie, the waistcoat, I just had no control at all. I played in the plate competition but I had no interest. About the only good thing about getting knocked out is that you get to sit with all the losers and listen to the stories. But then you drink so much that the stories start to make sense because they start to sound as true as your own.

Around this time, I was pretty much unattached. When I was resident professional on the Riley stand at the Ideal Home Exhibition in March 1974 I met a girl who came up to the plate competition at the world championship. We went to a restaurant and a little Spanish guy came over singing "My darling, I love you," and all the rest of it. She just got up, picked him up and stood there with him. He was still playing the guitar looking up at her face. I figured she might have been a little too strong for me. It also made me feel a bit of a wimp because there was no way I could have picked the guy up.

Eddie Charlton invited me to play in a Victorian Masters in Melbourne. It was just single-frame matches with a two-frame final on aggregate score but I ended up winning it, beating Spencer in the final. In an interview afterwards, John said: "The way Cliff played tonight proved that he is really the up-and- coming player in the world today".

I was really choked. I was so pleased. I had started to play my own game and I was enjoying it. My long potting was still very poor but I wasn't getting screwed up by the nap and I was getting a lot more confidence. I could sense when I played somebody that just by their choice of shots they were showing me a lot more respect than they were before.

I was accepted as a good fighter. My big problem at the time was that I did not have many opportunities to gain experience. I still had only played in about a dozen tournaments in my life. When you're playing for money, it's the easiest thing in the world because you can always go back the next day and beat the guy. When you're playing in a tournament, the pressures on because, if you lose, that's it, see you next year. It was difficult to gain confidence and I was also going wrong often when I was playing safety because I almost wanted to tie the guy up with a rope and put a blindfold on him, just completely tie him up. You can't do that all the time. You can end by tieing yourself up.

After this Victorian Masters, John Pulman and I were asked to do about six or seven shows so we stayed on for about another month. This was where I started to learn how to drink. The first deal that we had, John and I were the guest speakers at, I think, the Danish Sportsmen's Club in Melbourne. I had my speech all planned and John and I were sat there at the top table. There were maybe 60 guys there but as the time approaches I start to panic and I realise I've completely forgotten what I was going to say.

By the time the MC is announcing the speakers I didn't know my own name, why I'm there or where I was but, fortunately, I'd had a very large amount of wine. This has changed me so much that as the guy's announcing a speaker I'm so disappointed that it isn't my turn that I'm almost tugging at the guy's shirt because I'm so eager to start talking. Finally, when I do get up to talk I start telling some stories about being in San Francisco and on the road and amazingly this guy said in the papers next day that I was as funny as Bill Cosby. Then John got up and told a few jokes and then we had to go downstairs and play one frame of snooker. The highest break was eight.

This wasn't so bad because it was meant to be a social occasion but by then it was four in the afternoon and John and I had to do an exhibition that night. We were in no state for this. I thought that John, with his vast experience of being pissed, would save the day but I was wrong. I broke off and left John this long red, about half ball. He missed the ball completely. All that you could see was the cue ball going past the red, hitting the top cushion, coming back through the reds, going between the brown and green, back out between the brown and yellow, up the table through the reds to the top cushion, and back down the table through the reds.

We hit the ball about once more each and I could hear the comments: "Look, they're pissed". It was very bad. What happened was that I had to go back there about a month later and put on a free show for them but the next day the guy who had compared me to Bill Cosby in his paper wrote: "Cliff Thorburn and John Pulman knocked them dead at the Northwood Club last night". Needless to say, he hadn't been there.

When we played our next show about three days later, the word had got round. We had a fantastic reception when we were introduced but when I went to sit at the players' table there was a large bottle of scotch on it. Actually, we had three centuries in four frames so this rescued our reputations a little. It was just a bit unfortunate that we had got caught at the sportsmen's lunch.

In late-August 1974, there was a tournament at the Canadian National Exhibition Centre in Toronto. It was run by Terry Haddock, of Snooker Canada, and was held annually for the next seven years with modest prize money. In 1974, the first prize was $1,500 (£651) but almost every Canadian of note played in it because it offered a chance to compete against world class opposition. Several British players travelled over, partly because they could treat it as a holiday.

Invariably it was boiling hot. Every year except one, the snooker tournament was held in the Automotive Building on a first floor overlooking a fashion show and various displays, most of them with musical accompaniment or in the case of a police display, a siren. The air conditioning generator whirled noisily all day without much reducing the heat. There was no admission fee so the public walked up to see the snooker as they might earlier have watched the lumberjacking display, the agricultural show or the numerous other attractions. There were always full houses for the best matches.

Dennis Taylor made a name for himself in practice for the event by making 349 without missing. He cleared the table in the first frame with a break of 103 and fluking a red from the break-off, compiled a total clearance of 134 in the second. His opponent broke in the following frame and Taylor made 112 first visit.

Taylor reached the final of the tournament by beating Higgins 8–6 and led 5–3 at the interval of the final before Cliff won 8–6. Cliff had early beaten Willie Thorne 8–6 and Graham Miles 8–5. *Snooker Scene* reported that after their match, Dennis said: "On his own tables, Cliff is red hot. All he needs is one chance."

I've got a big edge when I play at home, especially in front of a big crowd. When we came out on the final night, there was this maze of people, an extraordinary number of them. When Dennis was introduced first, the ovation he got you just wouldn't believe. When I came out, they were all standing up and wouldn't sit down. I had to keep my hands by my side because, if I raised them, I felt that I'd start shaking and wouldn't be able to stop. When I got to the table, I felt like I couldn't even hold my hands by my side because I was shaking so much. I had to start wiping my cue. I had to do something. It seemed like I wiped it for ten minutes. I was sure someone was going to shout: "It's clean, Cliff," or "It's dry for God's sake".

This is probably one of the most important things that ever happened in my life and to this day I still don't understand it. When we shook hands, we were both nervous but I went down to break the balls and as I put my hand on the table, I was calm. Everything was still.

My grandmother died during the tournament. Just afterwards I had to do a TV commercial and then go home to her funeral next day. Then the TV commercial was put back a day and I had a problem. I was torn between going home for the funeral and doing something which was very important for my career. At that time hardly anybody in Canada knew me except for the snooker people and this was a chance to move up a league. I agonised about it and eventually I did the commercial. It made me feel bad, but I felt as if I was in a no-win situation. I had actually been trying to give up smoking and had been doing pretty well for a month but the next day I started again. For the commercial I played a massé round a beer bottle and the commercial got in the top ten in North America.

A few weeks later I was in Vancouver at my mother's place when a guy phoned me up. I knew the call was from a long way away because I heard about 30 coins go in the box. The voice said: "My name's Chris Keogh from Mouth Polasky, Illinois. I hear you're a snooker player." He wanted to arrange some matches for money so I went down to Mount Polasky with Wayne (Simpson) and we won two or three thousand dollars. Then we went up to Detroit looking for Cornbread Red. He's called The Rooster because he has red, slicked-back hair. He wears cowboy boots and a cowboy shirt and he's truly one of the greats down there.

We played snooker and Red had me down to my last $100. We'd lost maybe $2,000. We were playing on a five foot by ten with an oversized cue ball with three reds. It took me a little while to get used to it. It took me $2,000 in fact.

I said to Wayne: "I guess I've gotta smarten up. I'll be back in stroke in a couple of games."

Wayne said: "You have to be back in stroke in this game."

"Why's that?"

"We'll go broke."

I proceeded to get all my money back plus we broke the whole joint. As I'm making my come-back, as I'm getting into Red's pocket so to speak, I've been noticing that Red's backer was hanging his jacket up every 15 minutes or so on this old toilet door which is only on one hinge. Somebody would come by and give him some money and then they would go over to the jacket and pull out some drugs or something.

Anyway, we played on and I'm starting to go through Red very, very easily. He's absolutely gone and his backer said in a strange high voice: "I deal in dead bodies and pussy and I hate to see my Rooster lose".

We had to have somebody walk with us out to the car and when we went down side streets we had to make sure that no one was following us. For situations like this Wayne had bought a tin of Mace, like postmen have to deal with troublesome dogs. It's some stuff which makes your eyes go red. Anyway, we got back to the hotel with this $6,000 which was a lot of money in 1974. We threw it all up in the air and it seemed like it didn't come down for about five minutes.

Then we went to Ottawa for the Canadian championship where I played Julien St. Denis in the final. It was best of 25, 10 frames in the afternoon and 15 at night. Yes, 15. You don't want 15 at night with me, I tell you, not if you want any spectators! He was ahead 10–5. I beat him 13–11 and we finished at four o'clock in the morning. So that match with Griffiths in the 1983 world championship was an early night compared with this. At 4.30 in the morning there was still 250 people there, all drinking beer.

Next day, we were just leaving Ottawa and we stopped at this gas station to fill up. There was a dog barking so I said to Wayne: "Why don't we try that Mace?" He squirted it but all that came out was this thin stream of bubbles. I could've just seen ourselves in Detroit if we'd tried to use it. "Stand back," we'd have said, and then out would have come the bubbles.

I went over to England for the second Norwich Union Open. I had just had an Afro haircut and I wore a brown check suit. I was beating Fred (Davis) 3–1 at the interval. It was a few minutes before I came into the players' room and there was Fred asleep in his chair. I just couldn't believe it. It sort of got me. Fred won the next three frames and then I won the last two to win 5–4. I got over a major hurdle there because Fred was definitely in the top eight in the world at the time.

After I'd beaten Fred, Jacob de Vries came up to me and said that he thought my hair was disgusting, and that if I don't get it cut then I can't play in the tournament. I didn't get it cut, because I really resented this guy. My hair was nice and tidy. I had a North American style suit on and North American haircut. I wasn't going to have it parted down the middle and all slicked back. Who gives a damn about my hair? I'm the guy who's come over from Canada. I got a little bit fired up. I tried to play harder and not lose my concentration. Pulman was in front of me 3–1 and I won the last four.

I was playing John (Spencer) in the semi-finals and I was 5–1 up. I was playing well and John was playing very well. It was about 7–7 when I noticed Margot (Spencer) sat in the front row. I looked over and she gave me what I thought was a dirty look because I was winning or something and I just lost my concentration. I thought: "What the hell's going on here? How important is this frame? Crumbs, this is really important." Very poor thinking. I lost the last two or three frames.

I felt like I shouldn't win. I was trying like hell but my concentration went. I was young. I had no experience. I had no coach. I didn't have any driving force behind me. I just had to do it all by myself and I was thinking: "I wouldn't be here if it wasn't for John". So my concentration just went. I don't know how. I think more than anything I got mad at Margot for not smiling at me although I know she didn't *have* to smile at me.

Early in 1975 I played in the Benson and Hedges Masters at the New London Theatre. I lost to Pulman 5–3. I don't remember too much about the match but what I do remember is that I got £125 for it and here is Jacob de Vries again saying that he thought I should stick around for the sponsor's benefit for the next five days. I had to pay my own hotel and all my expenses and I thought: "What the hell's going on here?"

The 1975 world championship was in Australia. Eddie Charlton promoted it. Although we played on a Starline table, which I absolutely detested, I played excellently against Paddy Morgan and beat him 15–6. I played Graham Miles next and beat him 15–2. Graham was quoted as saying that he lost because his tip came off. I'm convinced that I would have beaten anybody in those two particular matches.

I lost to Eddie in the quarter-finals, 19–12, but we were 11–11. We were playing in Brisbane. It was very, very hot. They had the cooler fans going and one time I stuck my cue up in the air and the fan was so low I scraped the side of my tip with it. I could have cut my cue in half.

Our last session was at two o'clock in the afternoon with Eddie ahead 13–11. There was no air conditioning, just these fans going round. It was 90 degrees. All of a sudden, Eddie, who I had started to grind down a little bit – my safety was becoming better than his – started to speed up. He went for everything. He hardly missed a thing. He was running around the table, running round it. Eddie Charlton! I don't think that anybody has played better than he played those seven frames against me. He just beat me up.

I knew that Eddie was going to come close to winning the championship. He won convincingly against Dennis Taylor 19–12, in the semis. I didn't see the final but I had a sizeable bet on Eddie so I wasn't too pleased when Ray (Reardon) won the first seven or eight frames. Then Eddie got in front 24–16 and I'm thinking in terms of champagne all round and then Ray's won it on the last game 31–30.

Obviously, of all the overseas players, Eddie probably deserved to win the world championship before me because he was very close a few times, but I could never understand why he plays the way that he does. It took me a while to realise that sometimes I've got to stick my neck out even when I know that I don't like the shot. I've seen Eddie do exhibitions and he can thump them down the cushions, play with side and do everything a top player is supposed to do, but he will not break away from that narrow mould of his when it matters. I just can't understand why he didn't change his game at the right time. I would guess that he must have played all his shots against Ray and then tried to protect his lead.

As for myself, I wasn't too upset at having lost to Eddie because he had played so well. It was only my third season on the circuit but I was really starting to play and my confidence was becoming world class.

Back home, I lost to Bill Werbeniuk for the North American championship in Toronto. Both of us knew that I was playing better than Bill at the time and, although I wanted to win, I didn't want to beat him really badly. There was nothing much going on at home so when we did have a match it needed to be something to give people an appetite for other matches.

I practised with him three days beforehand and I'm almost helping Bill get his game in shape. I also did a very stupid thing. We got into a screw shot competition and I beat him for $50, but my arm ached so much from playing all those power shots that when the match began I couldn't pot a ball. By that time, Bill had got in stroke and he was all over me. He was ahead 9–3. I won six in a row and then he won the last two to win it 11–9.

That was the last time the North American championship was held so Bill has been able to bill himself as North American champion ever since. He could have the longest reign since Queen Victoria. The other thing that sticks in my mind about that tournament was the tickets. Bill's name was spelt correctly but somehow or other mine was printed as Cliff Thornebury. That made me feel real good.

The main problem was that there were fewer opportunities in those days so it was harder to make them count. There were a few things here and there. I once played Kenny Shea a week's match in Halifax, Nova Scotia. I had a bad cold and I was sucking a cough candy. I coughed and the candy flew out all over the balls. I guess this must have been a foul. It also made the balls very sticky.

Bob Paquette and Paul Meaney always treated me very well in Montreal and helped me get shows there. Bob has done a tremendous amount for the game, particularly on the amateur side. He got to the world amateur quarter-finals in 1978 – Kirk got to the semi-finals – and he got to the final of the Canadian championship four or five times in the Seventies when most of the Canadian professionals were in it. Bob did all this while having a very responsible job as a negotiator with the Port of Montreal Authority. Bob Hargrove, who had a small room in St. John, New Brunswick, would book me whenever he could.

I didn't play in a big tournament until the next year's world championship, 1976, when I lost 15–14 to Higgins. He also beat John Spencer on the last game and Eddie Charlton 18–16 in the semi and I felt that I'd probably played better against Alex that year than John or Eddie had. I was ahead 14–12 and lost the last three games. I remember Alex making a couple of flukes and making 50 or 60 off them. I did have a chance in the last game but I fluffed it. I was tight on the rail with a red over the corner pocket so it wasn't all that easy, but those are the sort you've got to get. Even so, I felt I was good enough to win the championship. As it was, Reardon won it – again.

Snooker Scene's report of Cliff's match against Higgins is worth recalling.

Alex Higgins 15 Cliff Thorburn 14

Scores: 58(29)–41; 105(25,40,36)–7; 31(25)–71(30); 87(36)–14; 42(30)–68(24,44); 80(51)–6; 30–107(36,50); 70(24)–50(32); 28–67(48); 14–86(20,62); 43–79; 46–58; 53–93(87); 76(56)–47(28); 61(22,27)–58(24,24); 18–8(47,23); 37–71(22,32); 79(23,30)–42(31); 103(67,27)–37; 88(38,41)–24; 25–58; 66(43)–78(40); 7–72(22,31); 73(65)–28(27); 72(26)–10; 29–72(68); 100(48,52)–36(36); 79(54)–23; 92(38,32)–38.

Higgins won the last three frames from 12–14 to win this marvellously exciting match after Thorburn had done everything that he could have been expected to do to achieve what the general public would have regarded as a surprise win, but which those on the inside of snooker would have regarded only as confirmation that this likeable Canadian is genuinely world class.

Higgins won the first session 4–2 but Thorburn played superbly to win six of the eight evening frames to lead 8–6 overnight, his 87 clearance in the penultimate frame, in which many balls were on or near cushions, rightly bringing the house down.

On the resumption, Thorburn took a good long last red in the first frame but missed the black from under the cushion which would have left Higgins needing snookers and the Irishman took the colours to win on the black to pull back to 7–8. Thorburn won the next two but Higgins worked up an irresistible momentum to win the last three frames of the session, a favourable run of the balls supplementing his good form and breaks of 30, 67, 38 and 43.

Thorburn then won the first three frames of the evening session to lead 13–10, the second of these in incredible fashion after Higgins, in play with 43 and needing only to roll the blue from its spot into the middle pocket to win, had incredibly left it on the lip of the pocket for the Canadian to clear the table. It seemed impossible that Higgins could win after such a blunder but a 65 break got him going again in the 24th frame and a 72–10 win in the next brought him to only one behind.

An immaculate 68 showed that Thorburn had not cracked, but the closing three frames were to see Higgins roar in like a tidal wave which mere skill could do nothing to check. Thorburn is a popular player but the support for Higgins was overwhelming. The crowd seemed happier to say "hard luck" than "good shot" for the Canadian's efforts while each ball that Higgins potted was greeted almost with acclamation.

Higgins, chancing his arm, benefited from two outrageous flukes in the 27th frame, in which he made breaks of 48 and 52, and started a 54 break in the 28th frame with another fluke which brought an approving roar and an amazing single cry of "salubrious – yes" from the back of the hall. After an early 38 by Higgins in the decider, Thorburn fought back with a 21 but was always struggling and a fantastic thin safety shot from Higgins, slipping the last red behind the black, led to the Irishman, like a matador making the kill, compiling a triumphant clinching 32.

FIVE

WORLD CLASS

THE WORLD at large knew nothing of Cliff's current form going into the 1977 Embassy World Championship. He was not invited into the ten-man field for the 1977 Benson and Hedges Masters, and in the so-called World Matchplay Championship in Australia, playing with a cue whose joint had worked irreparably loose, he had lost 15–6 to Gary Owen. In those days, only eight players qualified as of right for the 16-man field for the competition for the Embassy World Championship which that year was staged at the Crucible Theatre, Sheffield, for the first time. In the qualifying competition Cliff easily beat Chris Ross, but it did not give any realistic assessment of Cliff's championship chances. Methodical and sure, Cliff beat Rex Williams 13–6 at Sheffield with 74 and 70 as his best breaks, but it was his 13–12 quarter-final win over Eddie Charlton with which he really came of age as a championship contender.

I really relished the last couple of games. I always have enjoyed that type of situation. I played a guy called Legau in Montreal in 1970. I had to give him 20, one red. I had lost all my money and I'm playing the next game on my nerves so to speak. It goes to a re-spotted black. The fellow pots the black and goes in-off and then I beat the guy for all his money. So I've never had that fear of the last game. The 15th round or the last hole or something like that is what turns me on. Even at golf, I love to have a 12-footer on the last green for the money.

When I played Eddie that time, it was the first time in Britain I felt that I had a second game. I felt I could play without giving up anything. The fellow might knock in a good shot and beat me, but I could play without giving anything up. Everything was a nice feeling. Sometimes, when you're playing bad, you feel like you're still but the room's moving but, when you're really playing well, everything's still and your concentration is good.

I didn't think Eddie could win the last game. I'd never felt that way before even though I'd had some success. I really felt that I could shut him down completely like Reardon used to all the time. The last game was 61 minutes but it was still good snooker. That's the way you have to play in the world championship.

Cliff Thorburn 13 Eddie Charlton 12

Session 1: 65–43; 32–75(54); 66–46; 80–27; 41–75(54); 64–71; 76–17; 71–52; Session 2: 44–77(43); 62–59; 29–71(30, 32); 60–57; 22–75(31, 38); 23–78(49); 75(52)–17; 77–23; Session 3: 49–76(52); 41–86(31); 59–62; 104(69, 35)–5; 55–46; 55(43)–80(37); 50–56; 68(46)–54(53); 105(40)–14.

I beat Dennis Taylor in the semi-finals, 18–16. We were 16–all. It was like the 1980 final against Higgins: in the penultimate frame I made a century with the black right out of it and then the last frame I shut him out. In 1973, I'd given myself a goal of five years to get to the final of the world championship. If I'd given myself a goal of five years to win it, I might have won the world championship twice by now but I was so happy just to get there.

Dennis Taylor in action at the Canadian National Exhibition in 1977. This was in the days when he made it a little easier for us by not wearing glasses. Joe Davis, still immaculate with the temperature in the 80s, was an honoured guest that year. Bruce Donkin of Riley's, the table company, who has been a well known character on the circuit for a lot longer than I have, is seated between Dennis and Joe

Snooker Scene describes Cliff's progress through the semi-final to The Big One – the final

Cliff Thorburn 18 Dennis Taylor 16

Scores: Session 1: 96(57)–14; 14–89(50); 64–37; 79(50)–34; 87(52)–20; 25–91; 35–68. Session 2: 50–83(54); 36–67; 116(45, 36)–28; 43–92(63); 86(34, 34)–21; 20–98(43, 55); 84(37)–16. Session 3: 104(100)–16; 84(40)–41; 30–69(32); 44–62; 104(44, 57)–27; 79(53)–36; 68–61. Session 4: 21–100(39); 58(59)–66; 39–67; 61–44; 78(32)–38; 4(30)–54; 68–71(30). Session 5: 88(32, 30)–41; 38–76(39); 103(31)–22; 51–72(40); 111(111)–8; 98–30.

Within the inner circle of the game, it is regarded as a feat to reach a world semi-final but the less committed followers do not remember it very long – about as long as the losing FA Cup semi-finalists are remembered. A player who reaches the final, though, is at least part of The Big One. To two young players (both are 29) victory represents, apart from immediate considerations, an important breakthrough in status so it was not all that surprising that there were many nervous misses, particularly when one or the other was trying to consolidate an advantage.

Thorburn always looked the likelier winner but Taylor, who had gained confidence steadily during the championship, played with great heart and determination. His main technical fault, a tendency to snatch, surfaced in situations of extreme tension or when the cue ball was near a cushion but otherwise there was not much to criticise either in his technique or in his tactics. To have reached the semi-final twice in three years shows how near Taylor is to the top. Whether he can get there depends on eliminating that snatch and playing with more confidence when he has the initiative.

Thorburn led 4–1 but then lost the next four frames to trail 4–5. Taylor was again one up at 6–5 by virtue of an excellent 63 which contained several real pressure shots, and again at 7–6 before Thorburn levelled at 7–7. The third session began with a superb 100 from Thorburn notable for a remarkable cocked hat double of the last red. The Canadian led 9–8, missed an easy blue which would have put him 10–8, but managed to win the last three frames of the day to lead 12–9.

Taylor responded by winning the first three frames on the last day, the second after Thorburn had made a 49 break, to level at 12–12. Thorburn was also somewhat fortunate in the 25th frame when he made two terrible mistakes only to leave Taylor covered both times. These strokes of luck helped Thorburn to lead 14–12 but Taylor fought back with two black ball wins to level at 14–14.

When Taylor twice levelled after being the odd frame down in the final session, the second time when Thorburn missed a simple blue which would have put him two up with three to go, it seemed that the Canadian had had so many chances to win that he was incapable of doing so. This assessment proved to be entirely false for Thorburn reappeared from the mid-session interval to compile a clinical 111 clearance, potting his only black at the very end, before clinching the match by taking an 80–0 lead in the 34th frame, a run of 191 points without reply.

I felt good but the final was so long that I had highs and lows. The first session, against John Spencer, I lost the first three frames. George Crum had called me at five in the morning thinking it was three o'clock in the afternoon. He wasn't the only one who got the five hours' time difference the wrong way round. I was so naive that I didn't even tell reception that I wouldn't take any more calls after 11 p.m. I just couldn't wait to get to the last session. I didn't realise the importance of the middle of the match. If John got ahead, I pulled back. If I got ahead, he pulled back. It came down to the last couple of games of the penultimate session and I

The 1977 world final against John Spencer. He had a moustache that year and also became the first player to win the world championship with a two piece cue

knew they were important but I couldn't fire. I was down 22–20 and I lost the last session 4–1.

I had a friend with me, Tom Cawley from Victoria. He'd been with me down to San Francisco and Seattle and even when we'd had to go to the Canadian Embassy to borrow some money to get home. Years later, I was invited to a reception at the Canadian Embassy and I started by saying that I was there to repay a debt because the Canadian government never did get back the $5 they lent me.

Anyway, Tom was in Sheffield and he wanted to have a bet. He had about £1,000 to put on me. I was big odds but when we walked into the shop they were straight on the phone – with head office I suppose – and they said that the best odds they could offer were 5–1. Tom was with me right through the tournament and he kept on at me: "Grind, grind, grind". Halfway through the final, I felt I was getting bogged down by all the grinding and that I had to go for some shots. When we got back to the hotel that night, he was on at me: "Jesus, what are you doing out there? Grind, grind."

Then I've got one or two of the players saying to me: "Loosen up, play a bit open". I didn't know what the hell to do. Plus I was overawed. I was totally inexperienced and to the British public, the bad guy. I could feel myself slipping. It was a horrible feeling. I don't think it was through nerves but it was all just a bit too much for me. Years later, I saw some film of the final frame. There was a shot where John had me in awful trouble and I just stood there for about five or six minutes looking at it. There was only one shot to play and finally I did play it, but I was just standing there as if I was hoping that if I stood there long enough, they'd start the match over again.

THE FINAL

John Spencer 25 Cliff Thorburn 21

Scores – Session 1: 63–49; 98(38, 30)–21; 79–24; 41–46; 28–94; 73(30, 33)–13. Session 2: 70(68)–46; 39–77(37); 11–72(37); 29–64(33); 87(75)–21; 32–70(33, 30). Session 3: 41(35)–90; 51(36)–62(30, 31); 84(54)–40; 105(97)–21; 4–69; 118(105)–0. Session 4: 60–71(32)–31; 73(3)–45; 33–85(44); 53–85(58); 38–70(38). Session 5: 38–58; 48(47)–77(77); 87(41, 39)–31; 90(41)–40; 81(32, 41)–20; 63–68. Session 6: 29–82(45); 59–26; 78(78)–58; 70(44)–44; 39(34)–75(75); 46–85. Session 7: 93(37)–20; 64–51(34); 74(35)–21; 9–89(58); 36–72; 107(67)–20. Session 8: 17–74; 83(43)–14; 69–36; 72(51)–12.

It was less than ideal from Thorburn's point of view to have to start the final less than 12 hours after completing his semi-final. Indeed, it could be argued that the 3–0 lead which the fresh Spencer took while his opponent was finding his bearings was to prove decisive. The Canadian did make a partial recovery in the first session to drop it only by a 4–2 margin and recovered in the afternoon from 2–5 to 5–5, a controversial decision by referee John Smyth contributing to Spencer's loss of the 10th frame.

Apart from one referee who did not survive the first week, the refereeing was good but it is in the nature of things for one mistake to be noticed after any number of sessions have passed without incident. With the cue ball touching one red near the pack, Spencer potted another and split the bunch open only for the referee to call a foul on the grounds that Spencer had moved the touching ball. Spencer calmly pointed out afterwards that it would surely have been impossible to have potted the red if he had in fact disturbed the touching ball, but there was little doubt that this cost him the frame.

Level at 6–6 at the second interval, Thorburn went into the lead for the first time by winning the first two frames of the evening session, the latter with a cool clearance of the last two reds and colours up to the pink. Spencer responded, when trailing 30–40 in the following game, by digging in a good long red and running to game with a break of 54 to prevent a three frames gap opening. A 97 clearance then enabled Spencer to level at 8–8 and a great session ended with the last two frames being shared, the last producing a 105 to Spencer which began when the Canadian missed the easiest of slow reds.

The fourth session was Thorburn's 4–2. Spencer was particularly ill at ease in the last frame of the morning when he was in three times without being able to kill the game, though he almost pulled the penultimate frame out of the fire when trailing by 40 points with only the colours remaining, a combination of penalties and free balls putting him in a position to win before he went in-off the green in playing a safety shot. Thorburn extended the three-frame winning streak with which he had ended the morning to five by winning the first two frames of the afternoon to lead 15–11. It seemed that a gap was about to develop but Spencer hung on and with Thorburn faltering won the next three to go only one behind.

The last frame of the session was a classic. Spencer led 50–4 but Thorburn, coolly taking eight balls for 17 with the black hanging over the pocket, recovered with this and a later 30 to get a shot at the pink for game before Spencer won on the black to level at 15–15.

The second evening's session was another to savour. Thorburn led 16–15 and after Spencer had levelled again looked like recapturing the lead when he led 58–0 in the third frame only for Spencer to clear up with 78. Spencer went on to lead 18–16 and led 34–0 in the following frame but this time it was Thorburn's turn to respond with a winning 75 and go on to take the last frame of the day to reach 18–18.

On the last morning, Spencer rose at 7.30 – not a familiar hour for him – for an hour's stroll in the park to get his mind clear for the struggle ahead. The crucial first frame was scrappy but Thorburn's mistakes were the more serious and Spencer was again able to go one-up. With the tension really biting, Spencer made only seven with all the balls open and Thorburn six. Spencer, 34 in front with only one red left, had a reasonable shot at it for game and refused it in favour of safety. Thorburn had the better of the safety exchange and made a cool 28 but lost position for the black and had to attempt it from long distance. He caught it too thick and Spencer steadied himself to put it away 20–18.

With Thorburn finding that he had to commit himself to shots which had serious consequences if he missed, the third frame also slipped away from him to give Spencer a 21–18 lead. The Canadian won the next two to reduce his deficit to one and was first in in the last frame of the session only to miss a black off the spot. "I should be used to these balls by now but it just crossed my mind as I was playing it whether I could hold position for the next red just by running through it or whether I needed a touch of running side," he said. This moment of indecision cost him dear, in the form of a 67 break from Spencer and a 22–20 lead. Thorburn recovered to only one behind but that was his last effective resistance. Spencer compiled an excellent 43 to win the following game, drew steadily away to win the next and produced a 51 which gave him a lead so commanding in the concluding frame that Thorburn conceded with two reds left.

I won £2,000 and I went back home and bought a car, the first I'd ever owned. I was 29 years old and I had never driven before. Well, actually, I had but I hadn't had a licence. I'm the epitome of procrastination. I just let things go. I had this car so my friend Wayne Simpson thought we were ready for a tour across Canada. I guess we stopped at every town we thought could hold an exhibition in the local billiard room. We drove all across Canada to Vancouver, booking all the shows as we went, spent two weeks in Vancouver and worked our way back. I'd do a show and we'd drive 400 miles through the night to do another one. It finally caught up with us because we did miss one show. We were just too late so we drove through town at midnight with our heads down and collars turned up. I played 23 shows in 22 days and drove 2,800 miles. We had a hell of a time and we got a great reception at all these places.

We played at Banff Springs in the Rocky Mountains which has a Canadian Pacific hotel and a golf course. I played golf in a yellow shirt and the black fly they have up there love yellow. I had bites all over me. I looked like the Elephant Man. Two hours later, I was playing snooker and Wayne was doing one of his marvellous intros. It was about 95 degrees.

Everywhere we went we had press and TV, an amazing amount of it considering it was such a fly-by-night operation. There still is tremendous potential for somebody like me to be sponsored to go across Canada, maybe by a brewery, in the winter. We even got up to Moose Jaw in Saskatchewan. It was 108 degrees outside and we played in a basement with no air conditioning, packed with 350 people. We played in two rooms in Winnipeg and then at this golf course at Jekyll Island which was about a 150-mile drive.

The idea was to drive back, sleep in Winnipeg and then hit Thunder Bay in the morning. But I had a flat tyre and with the type of car I had you needed a special type of wrench. The wrench broke. We got back at about four o'clock in the morning and slept in a hotel for about an hour and a half. I was going to fly to Thunder Bay because there was a plane at 7.30 in the morning but I missed it. I'm right at the door of the aeroplane, right there, but they closed the door. Bang, that's it.

So we'd got 440 miles to do in ten hours. We drive 250 miles like maniacs to a place called Kenora because a plane goes from there to Thunder Bay. We're opposite the airport and I get a speeding ticket. So exactly the same thing happens. I get there just as they are towing the steps away. I never phoned the people to say I'd be late because I was so embarrassed. That was where we drove through town at midnight.

We lived well. We stayed in the best hotels. We had a lot of fun. I made a century break in every single show I played. I dropped Wayne off at his house and we broke dead even, charging about £150 a show. The next year, we did the same again. I had a century break in every show except one, when I had a 99. I dropped Wayne off at his door and we'd broken even again. I said to him that there was no way I could let him go back into his house this time without any money so I gave him $20. We made no money but because I was playing so well I thought that this was the time that people should see me play. It made me more confident. I had no trouble doing the shows in front of the public. It was a great personal experience.

As for Wayne, he found something more profitable than managing me. He has a company with his brother which supplies tents which can be set up in 10 seconds and taken down in 15. Their biggest customers are Bell Canada who use them for the guys who have to go up telegraph poles.

In August 1977, I played in the Canadian Open but this year the permanent building it was usually held in had been booked by someone else so we played in a circus tent with three tables and seats for about 1,000 spectators. There was a plague of flies and it was well over 100 degrees in the tent. In the afternoon, the sunlight poured in and there was a steel band, a non-stop dance band and a circus in the next tents. The players all had a little smile when the master of ceremonies said at the start of each session: "I must ask you to be very quiet because the least distraction can upset the players".

The tables were raised on platforms four or five inches from the ground. There were miles of cables underneath them for the lighting. One day, we had a cloud-burst and there were all these cables under water and all these people sitting on metal bleachers. I lost 9–6 to Higgins in the quarters and he won the tournament.

Around this time, a few events were getting going in England. Naturally, if it had been on merit, I would have been in all the tournaments – except for some events which were on invitation and the promoters felt that they would prefer somebody who was a more obvious crowd-puller. I could understand that, even though I would have liked to have played in everything. This was also the first year of the UK championship, which is open to everybody now but which at the start was restricted to British players. I thought maybe that it should have been open right from the start because it was excluding just a few overseas players. On the other hand, I didn't want to spend all my time in Britain anyway.

I went to Japan with Spencer who was going to see Dick Helmstetter about a cue contract. Dick founded Adam Custom Cues and knows just about everything there is to know about making cues. John and I had adjoining rooms on the top floor of the Hilton. We were both shaving when we heard a rumble like a gravel truck going by. Then it sounded like about 30 gravel trucks going by. Then, all of a sudden, the whole building starts to shake. I thought: "Let's go". But where? I was so scared but it just got worse and worse. I was looking at the walls and one of the top corners just changed shape. Then it all stopped and John came into my room looking as if he'd just been hit by Muhammad Ali. His legs were gone and I must have looked the same. We went downstairs and the head porter told us it was the worst earthquake they'd had in years.

I didn't play a tournament in England in the 1977–78 season until the Benson and Hedges in January 1978. I beat Doug Mountjoy, who was the holder, 4–2 – this was when we played best of seven in the early rounds – and in the semi-finals I beat John Spencer 5–3. At 3–3, I was 0–50 and cleared up to win on the black. I was getting sick and tired of thinking he was special. Right from when I first knew him and Ray, it seemed that they had certain qualities which they'd just been born with but, of course, these had only come from experience. I had won in Australia and won in Canada, but it was starting to beat me down that I hadn't won in England. I was ready to win, but I didn't this time because I lost 7–5 to Higgins in the final. I could have gone ahead 6–4. There were three reds in a cluster. I went for the break out off the black and missed the black. I lost my momentum right there but I felt I was knocking on the door and as if just one good shot might make the difference.

I went to Sheffield in April feeling that I was playing well enough to win the world championship. I beat Patsy Houlihan 13–8 and then lost to Eddie Charlton from four up with five to play. I just wish that Willie Thorne hadn't lost to him from three up with four to play the round before because he talked so much about it. At 12–9, I was 40 in front. I was on the side cushion and I played a red sticking out from a pack of four. I missed it and Eddie cleared up.

The next game, I trapped him so that he was tight on the baulk cushion, just out from the baulk pocket. He couldn't get safe and he couldn't get on anything. He just rolled the red in, smooth as silk, and put me in trouble. I got out of it and put him in the same situation that he'd been in before. But he just rolled that red in as well, pocket weight.

The whole thing just got worse and worse. The feeling came over me like a tidal wave that I was going to lose. I felt I just couldn't do anything about it. I've had that feeling a few other times since. You're regretting things that you did wrong that were silly or stupid and now you deserve to lose. If the particular shot that started it all off came up now I wouldn't shoot it. The shot was so totally out of character. I just got a little too confident.

To go from having a chance to win the championship to losing in a situation like that has got to intensify your self-doubt. I lost twice more in that situation in the Benson and Hedges Irish Masters and the Benson and Hedges Masters, both times to Higgins, but now I don't think about it. It's probably experience again. I just think: "Good, I'm four up with five to play".

That was a really bad day. I went back to my room at the Grosvenor to find that I had left my window open and that somehow a pigeon had come in and shit all over the bedroom. It was amazing how much had come out of that bird. I chased it all round the room and finally caught it and put it out of the window. I went to close the window, but it was a very heavy one of the old type. It caught me completely by surprise as it came down – bang. Two of my finger nails were absolutely black. They're throbbing with pain. What a day. I sat down in a chair and drank about half a bottle of vodka by myself and finally I started laughing.

A friend of mine, Bill Kavluk, had come over from Canada to see me win the championship, he hoped. He got to Sheffield just in time to see my last session against Eddie. He flew back next morning. Reardon won the championship – again.

I had a bad couple of weeks trying to sort myself out generally, but I had the summer off apart from my second tour across Canada with Wayne and then I won the Canadian Open by beating Tony Meo in the final 17–15 after being 10–6 down overnight. I got $6,000 for this. It was a surprise to a lot of people that Tony got to the final because he wasn't even a professional then and he had a real tough draw, beating some top players, including Higgins in the semis.

Round about the semi-finals, we all went to a disco. They had a dance contest on and Tony walked right in and won it. I was very impressed with Tony's game and I really thought that he would do much better than he has, but in some way he just seems to have let himself be overshadowed, perhaps because he was the No. 2 player in the Barry Hearn camp after Steve (Davis) and then just slipped down the list as Barry signed more players.

We also had a party at George Crum's. He had a swimming pool in his back yard and Rex Williams started to talk about John Pulman as a marathon swimmer. We can hardly believe this but Pulman says: "Let's bet" and eventually we dream up this contest where the loser has to buy this meal for about five of us at quite an expensive restaurant.

It was four lengths. Wayne is a very good swimmer and John is pissed. John goes in bang on his stomach and just sinks so Wayne is half way up the bath before John even gets started. Then John kinda loses his sense of direction and wanders over to the right- hand side of the pool before he gets to the end. Then he goes to the end of the pool and across to the other side, a bit like a three-cushion escape from a snooker. He's going back towards the middle of the pool again when he hits Wayne – bang! – right in the middle. By now, we're all helpless. We agree that John is the loser and Rex says: "It's been 25 years since I bet on you in a swimming contest, and it'll be another 25 before I bet on you again".

When boys like Tony Knowles and Joe Johnson came over from England they used to head either for Rocky's, which was a room that Rocky Manserra and Andy Diamond kept, or for Le Spot, where Gene Lew ran a Monday night tournament with six reds for about eight years with 60 or 70 guys in on a handicap basis.

One of the most likeable characters around at that time was a guy called Danny Campbell who's still in jail for embezzlement. In fact, he doesn't want to leave because there are so many guys who want to speak to him. In two years he probably lost $400,000. Guys were beating him for $25,000 and $30,000 in a night. I once gave him 60 start, best of nine for $500 and beat him 5–1. Afterwards he said:

"Christ, Cliff, you're so stupid. Why didn't you milk me?" He was great with finger spins but of course we wouldn't bet him on those.

Cliff's first appearance on the British circuit in the 1978–79 season was in the Holsten Lager International at the Fulcrum Centre, Slough, one of snooker's most complex and many sided disasters. The promoter, Ray Davies, was keen to try a new formula so early matches were contested on the aggregate score of three frames in the first round and six frames in the second and quarter-finals. Actually, this produced some remarkable results: Patsy Fagan started his last frame against John Spencer 91 in front only for Spencer to win with a break of 109; Rex Williams was 97 behind against Ray Reardon early in their last frame but won through with a 72 break and a green to black clearance.

On the other hand, the disadvantages of the system were epitomised by Cliff's own match with Spencer, for after three of their six frames, Spencer led 372–1. They had arrived a shade late, not for any scheduled time but because they were due to play the first three frames of their match after the six frames of Alex Higgins v David Taylor.

With no sign of the players, the crowd drifted away. Thames TV called a meal break for their crew. I was commentating for them that week so I, too, went across the road to Macdonalds. Cliff and John appeared and for no reasons best known to himself the promoter decreed that the match should start. There was a referee, a scorer and three or four spectators, including Graham Miles.

Too late, the news reached the TV producer of the day, the late Paul Lang, that there was action on the table. I met him coming out of the building as I was returning. "Spencer's made a maximum," he said. I realised instantly that this constituted a problem for the late-night highlights package. In fact, the 147 was not ratified as a world record. No one ever checked the pockets against the official templates and everyone was well aware that the middle pockets, in particular, were more generous than they should have been.

Troupers to the last, we put out the television highlights programme as scheduled with John obliging us by recreating the last few shots in the break, but it was hardly the same. One other unsatisfactory element of the event from a television point of view was that the promoter had neglected to obtain clearance from the local fire department about the distribution of seating to available gangways. No seats at all could be used on one side of the arena so television viewers obtained the strong impression that the venue was deserted except for some ghostly applauses coming from somewhere off camera.

Those people going off for a tea break was the most ridiculous thing I've ever heard in my life, but that's the way snooker was run at the time. After the first three frames, with me 372–1 down, I went back with John and Del Simmons to the Holiday Inn at Slough for a cup of tea. Del had started the International Snooker Agency with John and Ray Reardon. ISA managed Higgins. John and Del got this old lady to come over to me and say: "Are you Mr Cliff Thorburn?"

I said: "Yes".

"Are you the fellow that potted the red?" she asked.

It was the second 147 John had made on me. The first was in Edmonton when there was a £200 prize for the high run of the week which in 1972 was a lot of money. I had made a 144 but in the last session John made a 147.

A couple of weeks later I lost 5–4 to Perrie Mans in the Benson and Hedges Masters and he went on to win the tournament. At the interval, I was winning 3–1 and Perrie said to me that he had booked his flight home next day on an Apex ticket, which meant that he had to pay for it whether he went or not. I said that I had got to stay whether I won or not and that I hoped I'd win and then we'd all be happy.

We'd been playing five hours when it got down to 4–4 and I snookered him on the green. I thought that he wanted to go home real bad and that he would be quite happy to lose provided that he had given his best. I even thought that perhaps his heart wasn't in it. Of course, he flukes the green and clears up so now he's got this big problem with the air fare but I'm out of the tournament.

Around that time, Perrie beat a lot of good players and got to the 1978 world final but he lost form very quickly and almost overnight he started to lose almost every match he played. His strong South African accent sounds strange to Canadians at first, particularly the way he pinches his 'a' sound into an 'e'. This caught out one of the Canadian players, Frank Jonik, when he, Perrie and I were watching Silvino Francisco play shortly after he came on the professional scene. Silvino has an elder brother, Mannie – which a South African would pronounce 'Menny' – who was a very fine billiards player. We were stood there saying how well Silvino was playing and Perrie said: "He's an excellent billiards player as well. In South Africa he's second to Mannie." Up piped Frank: "Yeah, well, that's alright, but give us a ball park figure. How many?"

I've always felt that Perrie was lost over here. He was forever complaining about the tables being too fast. When I went to South Africa in 1979 I realised why. You were lucky to get 2½ lengths out of the club tables. I always felt that he was lonely and didn't really enjoy being here. I guess his father had been a national hero as far as snooker was concerned, South African champion and all that, and Perrie seemed to feel that he had to come over to England just because of that. He came over many times when it seemed like he didn't want to. He had a family torch to carry and it was a bit of a burden to him. But he's a genuinely nice guy.

I hung about for a couple of weeks after the Masters and then set off for what was supposed to be a trip to India and Australia, but I only saw India for a six-man round robin. I was still very nervous about getting on an aeroplane so I had four large scotches but when we were on the tarmac at Heathrow the plane is called back. We're not allowed to get off and we watch a mechanic stick a ladder up against the wing, lift the flap or whatever and poke around. He starts to shake his head and a second chap comes up. This one pulls out a little book and points to something in it. Then they start arguing. None of this is convincing me that flying is any safer than I thought it was so I'm just about falling apart when we eventually take off.

When we landed in Bombay we queued for 3½ hours to get through customs. I finished fourth in the tournament and Spencer won it. We were supposed to go on to Australia for a tournament Eddie Charlton was promoting, but this was cancelled so we were stuck another two weeks in Bombay. If it hadn't been for Dennis Taylor and Graham Miles I'd have gone crazy but these guys were just such fun. Near the end, when we had been together a month, they phoned me up in my room to say they had something very important to tell me. I rushed down to their room and the shower was going. They told me that there was a woman in there. This was very unlikely because young women are so strictly chaperoned in India. They went on winding me up until finally I've gone in for a peek and, of course, there's nobody there. That's 1–0 to them and that's okay.

Then Dennis started again. He and Graham were both sat on their beds with just towels on. "Listen Cliff, we've got something very important to tell you and you should have a drink."

I said: "Well, what is it?" And Dennis said: "Well, it's very important, you'd better have that drink."

Then he said: "Maybe you should make it a double". All this time he and Graham are just sitting there in their towels looking very solemn.

So I wolfed it back and said: "Well, what's up?"

Dennis said: "Well, Graham and I have been talking. We've been together now about four weeks and in fact both of us think we've fallen in love with you."

Game, set and match to them.

There was just nothing to do there. We had nothing to practise for so we were out partying but there were no girls. So one night Graham, Dennis and myself found ourselves on the dance floor dancing by ourselves.

Graham has a great sense of humour and a strange theory about money. He can explain that a 10p stamp is worth 50p. If you lose it, you have to buy another is how this theory starts.

We were once eating in Sydney and the bill came to $15.

I said to Graham: "Let's spoof for it".

He said: "Are you crazy?"

I said: "It's only $15".

He said: "No it's $75".

I said: "Jesus Christ, I'm gonna start eating for a living".

Graham is always trying to save money, not being cheap or mean or anything like that but because he has his own particular kind of shrewdness. He once had a car and the bonnet of it kept coming open so he had a guy weld the bonnet closed. He couldn't get into it or put oil into it or anything. He just drove the car into the ground.

At his peak in the mid-Seventies, Graham was a very good player but he got involved in a few businesses and his game lost its edge so he gradually slid down the rankings. It's sad really that he seems to be the forgotten man. It really disappointed me when they had *This Is Your Life* for Dennis that Graham wasn't there because he and Dennis were so close at one time.

After Bombay, I came back to England for the 1979 championship and lost to John Virgo 13–10. It was very important to me to beat this guy, but he played very well against me. His temperament was a lot better then. He played within himself a little bit and he was a slightly better player then than he was for five or six years afterwards. In the last couple of seasons, he's again started to play very well. I lost it with a pink in the last frame of the middle session which was probably one of the greatest shots I've ever seen. If I win the frame, I go in front 10–6, John needs the pink and black for it to be 9–7. The black is on its spot, the cue ball is tight on the top cushion and the pink is between the middle pockets and the baulk line just off straight.

It was surprising that Terry (Griffiths) went on to win it. His quarter-final against Higgins was a great match, but I flew home on the day the final started. I felt that Terry would win the final because he had the crowd on his side, overwhelmingly so, the Cinderella story almost.

Terry Griffiths duly won the world title at his first attempt by beating Alex Higgins 13–12 in the quarter finals, Eddie Charlton 19–17 in the semi-finals and Dennis Taylor 24–16 in the final. As I wrote in the introduction to Terry's first book, *Championship Snooker*: "On the table, Griffiths was perfectly self-possessed. Sitting out, he studied, when he sensed it was important, the game or his opponent; otherwise he sang soundlessly in his mind (often his favourite song, Myfanwy), or simply excluded everything from his cocoon of concentration, achieving a harmony of mind, in his inner game, which is the sportsman's optimum state. 'I was able to shut off completely from anything I didn't want. I've never done that, never, ever before'."

It often seems that a good player becomes a champion when certain elements in his life coincide. In Terry's case it appeared to be a time when his personal life was particularly happy. With a wife and two children to support, he had been dubious about sacrificing job security when he turned professional but he had just managed to overcome his immediate financial difficulties. The circuit was still new and magical to him and he was enjoying taking his father and his best friend, Peter Francis, to all his matches. He was living at home amongst all his friends and enjoying his practice without any of the demands which were to fall on him when he became champion. He was also, as a new professional, unencumbered by the weight of previous failures and thus was, in a sense, in a situation where he had everything to gain and nothing much to lose. Well as he has often played since, Terry has never quite recaptured his mood of April 1979.

But in the summer of 1979, Cliff's inward kaleidoscope was also settling in a way which was to help him win the 1980 world title. He had pursued his craft with utter dedication and single-mindedness and was ready to crystallise to best advantage this mass of accumulated experience. The player was ready but because life is always more than a series of snooker matches, the man needed some vital element, perhaps of reassurance or stability. In the summer of 1979, it was becoming clear that Cliff was going to marry Barbara Meaney.

SIX

WORLD CHAMPION

I MET BARBARA through her first husband, Paul Meaney, who's a snooker fanatic. Sometimes you have friends and you love them but without the desires and all that. As far as I knew, Barb's and Paul's situation was going quite well and I never would have done anything to harm it, but then they split up and Barb came down to Toronto in the New Year of 1979 to see some friends. We got together. She went back to Montreal but gave up her teaching job in June 1979 and moved to Toronto.

When she came down to Toronto, we knew that we were quite fond of each other. She was always very sports minded and always made me happy. If she had problems of her own, nobody knew about them. She always loved life and was good to be with. She is a happy-go-lucky sort of person and yet very well organised at the same time.

I went to South Africa in July for a tournament, the Limosin International, at the Good Hope Centre, in Capetown where I beat Rex Williams 8–7, after he'd been ahead 6–1, but lost in the semi-finals to Eddie Charlton 16–10. After the tournament I was invited to Durban with Rex and Carl Erasmus, who owns a big hotel there. Limosin had given us a jug of whisky which had been sealed for the flight but as my luggage was coming through I could see that it was dripping wet. The flight itself was the bumpiest I have had. I had Barb on one side of me and a pregnant woman on the other. They were both being sick into their bags at the same time.

We then drove to this game reserve about 200 miles away. The rhinos used to come right up to the door of the chalets. I came out one day and there was this rhino about 60 yards away and I'm about 35 away from the restaurant. I wasn't quite sure whether I could make it. I wouldn't like to have been wrong. I waited about an hour and by that time, of course, all the breakfasts had gone. When I finally got to the restaurant there was this huge ostrich just outside peering over the balcony. I went to touch him but it was obvious this was a big mistake. I took some pictures of the bison and the lions when they came up to drink and that was when I really realised that these were their natural surroundings and I was thousands of miles from home in the middle of Africa.

I'm glad I went to South Africa because it's a great place, but I've turned down all the invitations I've had to go back. There's no way I could condone what is going on in South Africa. All the South African sportsmen have got my sympathy but I believe that the sports boycott of South Africa is the best way of trying to change things. It's the only thing I can do anyway.

At the end of that summer I beat Terry 17–16 in the final of the Canadian Open after I'd been 10–3 in front. The atmosphere at the CNE was, as usual, nothing like the Crucible with the noise, the heat, the kids there with their balloons and everyone eating popcorn. One thing I'll never forget was a chap sat in the second row with his three kids. The game is on and this woman came down the aisle. She has her hands on her hips and she says to this guy, her husband: "Harry, Harry, get these goddam kids out of here. I wanna go home now. I've been here all day long and you've just sat here all day watching a snooker game. Come on, let's go." The guy's face! I felt so bloody sorry for him.

For all the distractions, it was tremendously satisfying to beat the world champion at home. It was very exciting and I was a bit fortunate in the final frame because he potted the blue, cannoned on to the pink and doubled it across into the other pocket. It was too bad that that match wasn't on Canadian TV rather than the 1980 final which was played under very primitive lights as well as all the other difficulties we always had at the CNE. I beat Terry 17–10 that time, but it was a poor match.

By the 1979–80 British season, the circuit was just starting to build up. The first tournament was the State Express World Cup which was at Haden Hill Leisure Centre near Birmingham. Outside Pot Black, it was the first short match type of experiment, and team snooker was completely new to the professional game. I think Bill, Kirk and I were the least selfish team in it and the most supportive of each other. We finished third of three in our group. I think that the sport needs an event like this and every year we still get excited about it. It's important that it stays in the calendar but England might not be the best place to have it.

The UK Championship, which John Virgo won that year, was still just for British players so the next tournament I played in was the second – and last – Bombay International, which was again a six-man round robin but this time with the top four going through to knock-out and semi-finals. In the round robin I beat Virgo 6–1 when he was really ill, but by the time I came to play him in the final, he was allright and I was really ill. I had to take some stuff for the "Bombay Tummy" that I had and one of its effects was that when I peed it came out blood red. I was stood in the gents with John just before the match and there I was pissing blood for all he knew. It even startled me a bit. He just grunted as if I was talking about the weather or something and this shows just how self-absorbed snooker players get. It was almost as if I could have been dying for all he cared and perhaps I'd have been the same if the circumstances had been reversed.

Anyway, he beat me 13–7 after I'd beaten Steve Davis 8–5 in the semis. Steve was in his second year as a professional and this was the first time I'd played him in

1980: Kirk Stevens, Bill Werbeniuk and I represented Canada in the World Cup as we did every year from 1979–1987

competition. I was nice to him afterwards because I really admired his play. I was so pleased to beat him that I said: " You stick at it, you'll be a hell of a player". As if he needed any encouragement! Even then, he was a hell of a player so when they bring up our record on TV or in the newspapers I get a bit irritated that this match seems to have been stricken from the record, perhaps because the Bombay tournament isn't in the circuit any more.

Just before the Benson and Hedges Masters in January 1980, I said to Barb that maybe we should live in England. She said that was fine if I thought it was going to help me. Then I said publicly that I thought I had to do this to win the world championship which, of course, turned out to be wrong. At the time, though, it seemed a good idea because I was just coming to England for a tournament and then going home and there was no continuity. I actually missed quite a lot of the British tournaments. Several of them were best of five or even shorter.

I beat Virgo 5–3 in the first round of the Masters, but I remember more clearly the previous day making a "16 reds" clearance in practice against Geoff Foulds at Neasden. I lost 5–3 to Terry in the quarter-finals and he went on to win the tournament. He was playing very well and he had a slow, even pace which he stuck to all the time. My own rhythm was still a little bit jerky unless I was playing really well.

73

Steve Davis in Canada in 1980, about three months before he won his first major title

Then, a couple of funny things happened. I was doing an interview after I'd lost to Terry when it was put to me that Eddie Charlton had said that he was going to be the first overseas player to win the world championship. I said: "No, I'm going to do it this year".

I said it without thinking, almost as a joke. Next day, I was in a restaurant just around the corner where we all used to eat and where a couple of nights before Terry had signed a plate "World Champion 1979". I was handed a plate and signed it: "Cliff Thorburn World Champion 1980". These predictions were coming out of me not because I was big-headed but because I was so relaxed, almost as if I knew I was going to win it.

In those days I never really had a base in England. Back home in Toronto I just practised or went out to the West Coast to play five or six exhibitions, which helped because I was playing in front of a crowd on strange tables. Mike Watterson has a club just down the road from the Crucible in Sheffield so this was the first year when I had somewhere convenient to practise. I felt that I had a lot of friends around Sheffield as well, which was not a feeling that I had about London. I had Barb with me and I went into the championship feeling very well prepared.

I went a week before the tournament without having a drink or a cigarette. I don't know what I was trying to prove exactly but I do know that it's not a good idea to change at such a moment something that's been part of your life for years. I stayed at the St. George and when I got up in the morning for my first match against Doug Mountjoy I walked around the trout pond in the gardens. Everything was beautiful and the birds were singing, but when I went out to play I was just a bloody mess. I couldn't stop shaking because I felt so nervous all of a sudden. I lost the first session 5–3 and I was lucky it was only 5–3 because I'd played like a complete idiot. I was so nervous I just couldn't control myself.

That night, everyone was playing cards and I stayed up until 4.45 in the morning. I had ten large Bacardi and cokes and got pissed out of my brains. When I woke up I felt pretty rough, but I had some coffee and soon I started to feel pretty good again. I showed up to play that afternoon and it was a complete reversal. In the first session nothing was happening, nothing was registering. The second session I won the first five frames and I got in front 9–7 which meant that I'd won that session 6–2.

Doug was quite a frustrating player to play then. He played hard. He didn't care if the pink and black were on both side cushions. Duggie has lost his hardness now and I have to a certain extent as well. I don't know whether that's old age or what although I find it makes snooker more enjoyable as I'm going for my shots. I won the first game in the final session to make it 10–7, but it got to 10–10 and I was still edgy. We'd had a 69-minute frame which included 21 minutes just on the brown and Duggie had won that to make it 10–8 and the next two as well. Then at 10–10 I won three close ones to win 13–10.

This put me against Jim Wych, who, about a month before in the Canadian championship, had beaten Kirk 9–7 in the semi-finals and came back from 0–4 against me in the final to 6–7. I only won the next frame on the black for 8–6 and beat him 9–6. In the qualifying round of the world championship, Jim beat Rex Williams 9–7 and at Sheffield, he beat John Pulman 10–5 and Dennis Taylor 13–10, so I knew how well he was playing. People have said that I had the Indian sign on him because I was the senior Canadian player and it was his first world championship and that because of all that he didn't really have it in him to beat me. But I didn't feel this way myself until near the end when I was on top and he could see it definitely slipping away from him. I led 5–3 at the first interval, then 10–6 and beat him 13–6.

I don't watch many matches, but I did happen to see the last frame or so of David Taylor's quarter-final against Reardon. The way Reardon was playing I guess I would rather have played him because, by his standards, he just wasn't playing at all. David played well in the last couple of games and won 13–11. I respected his ability but he's always had a really quick backswing which is difficult to play with under pressure so I did consider myself favourite. I won 16–7.

Higgins beat Kirk in the other semi-final 16–13 and then he led me in the final 5–1. I couldn't settle down and there was also some aggro when he said that I was standing in his line of sight and he put me off with clinking ice cubes into his glass of water. There I was, down on the shot, and I can hear this "clink, clink, clink." I said: "Please don't do that." I wish I had something that I really felt like saying. He was also coming to the table so quickly that I had no chance to get back to my seat without slowing him down so I would just get out of the way and stand by the cameras or something and go back to my seat after his first or second shot. There was one shot when I'm stood there, 15 feet behind him, and as soon as he struck the cue ball he's know that he's missed it. So immediately he turns round and glares at me. Then it got a bit nasty, not that this bothered me because I'd been through all that playing for money.

He was ahead 9–5 and he played a couple of flash shots and I've made it 9–9 at the end of the first day. I've had him in trouble and he's just thrown his cue at the ball so I thought it was a complete joke that he should say afterwards that I didn't win it but that he threw it away. My safety was good and I made 18 breaks over 40

My first match at the Crucible in the 1980 world championship aagainst Doug Mountjoy. We were both deadly serious but Snooker Scene used this as a caption competition. The winning entries included: "I see you've nosed in front again, Cliff" and "Doug's really hooked on this cue sniffing. He's gone rigid"

Kirk Stevens

in the final to his five. Barb and I both knew that I was going to win, especially when I got back to 9–9. I felt I had control all the time but there was a very bad moment at 16–15 when I missed a very easy brown off its spot which would have put me two up with three to play. Missing that brown came from nowhere. In spite of the tension of the match, I felt very loose, very good for the final session. I felt very tall as if I could look at the table from above.

When I actually missed the brown, I nearly died. I felt as if my whole body had turned into one big heart. Alex made it 16–16 and as I'm walking out to the loo after the frame a guy in the front row in a black tee shirt who's supporting Higgins says: "You've got him now. He's going out to be sick."

But there was no way I was going to let go at that stage. I made a 119 in the next frame and Alex hardly scored in the next and suddenly, after all those years, I was champion. It was very good to have Barb with me. She was very strong in the whole situation. In the final session, she was up in the players' room shouting for me, and Lynn, Higgins' wife, was naturally supporting Alex. At 16–16 Lynn walked into the players' room with a cake saying: "Congratulations. Year of the Hurricane. Alex Higgins, World Champion 1980". I thought Lynn and Alex were just perfect for each other. The cake was there when we all went out to Napoleon's that night. I had about six pieces of it.

THE WORLD CHAMPIONSHIP FINAL – SCORES

Cliff Thorburn 18 Alex Higgins 16

Session 1: 52–40; 46–55; 5–69(38); 47–61(32); 26–82(31); 18–98(93); 74(68)–31; 0–81(81); 62(62)–9 (Higgins 6–3). Session 2: 49(43)–61; 62(53)–58(54); 86(76)–27;

Barb and I cut the cake with Alex and Lynn after the 1980 World Championship

36–76; 45–63(41); 75(45)–17; 67(32)–45; 78(57)–38(32); 95(31, 64)–38(38); (9–9). **Session 3:** 86(41)–14; 60–21; 18–70; 27–93(47,45); 73(43)–43(34); 51–74; 115(58,35)–25; 61(42)–73; (13–13). **Session 4:** 21–67(34); 58–47; 100(35)–55(37); 53–55(36); 73(48)–41(40); 57–63(33); 119(119)–7; 96(51)–9.

Sometimes the achievement of a lifetime's ambition generates a euphoria which lasts for months. In these circumstances, success often begets success. But if the achieved reality soon starts to fall significantly short of the dream, if it becomes clear that one set of problems have merely been replaced by another, a player must almost feel as if he has been cheated of part of his prize. Cliff never described his feelings in quite that way but within months of winning the title, disappointments and problems, great and small, began to undermind his game, his confidence and his day-to-day peace of mind.

He did not receive the recognition as world champion that he had expected, or indeed that Terry Griffiths had received the previous year. He was and is well liked in Britain, but because much of his art is that which conceals art, because his outstanding virtues are unfashionably those of steadiness, consistency and determination, the British public did not take to him as they tend to take to players more flamboyantly skilled or more adroitly presented to the media by their managements. Within two years he slid from winning the 1980 world title to going from October to April in the 1981–82 season without winning a match.

Even though Cliff retained the Canadian Open in August 1980, the first disappointment was starting to crystallise. His capture of the world title was not going to do anything very much for snooker in Canada. This was how *Snooker Scene* saw it in its October 1980 issue:

CANADIAN OPEN SNOOKER: TIME TO MOVE ON FROM CNE

Every day some 200,000 people play snooker in Canada's 2,500 poolrooms, 150 of which are in and around Toronto and a thousand of which are two or three table set-ups in cafes. There are some 750,000 tables (including those in clubs and homes) in regular use. Snooker is booming but, paradoxically, it is making tortuously slow progress towards acceptance into sport's mainstream, an objective which British snooker, even after the most amazing decade in its history, is only just on the brink of achieving.

Cliff Thorburn's capture of the world professional title has made only a glancing impact in Canadian public consciousness in terms of a one-off success story rather than as an aspect of snooker's continuing activity. Thorburn's success attracted a number of newspaper profiles, a television documentary and helped clinch final day television coverage of the Canadian Open but neither the Canadian media not the Canadian public really regards snooker as bona fide sport along with golf and tennis.

Snooker is still seen almost exclusively in terms of a poolroom gambling activity. Its practitioners are socially suspect and its stars are acknowledged as such only by the game's vast sub-culture. Snooker is stuck with a disreputable image which will be improved only when the media takes serious notice of it.

This provides the clinching reason why the seven year-old Canadian Open should now move on from Toronto's Canadian National Exhibition Centre. CBC was persuaded for the first time to cover the final day's play but it is doubtful whether their coverage has enhanced the game's appeal to the uncommitted public.

A temperature in the 80s meant that Thorburn and Terry Griffiths, usually among the game's most immaculate dressers, felt obliged to discard their ties as marbles of sweat dropped from brow to table. The dress standards of the crowd were, understandably, casual in the extreme. But since the screen in the home does not convey heat, the pictures either created or reinforced the impression that snooker is played by young men in open neck shirts and watched by both sexes in jeans and tee shirts. One memorable figure opposite the black spot was resplendent in peaked baseball cap, black beard, overalls and singlet. We must remember to send him a ticket for the final night of the Benson and Hedges Masters.

A casual viewer might also gain the impression that snooker is habitually played to the relentless rhythm of the building's air conditioning plant or to the background of myriad lights from other attractions. If snooker is presented with no more dignity than a sideshow in a funfair, people will conclude that it is always like this and the Canadian press will be given at least some pretext for staying away – as they conspicuously did.

The Canadian Open had to start somewhere and to this extent the CNE has served a useful purpose but next year a more appropriate venue should be sought, possibly a hotel with an air conditioned ballroom. Hiring would be an expense but in return there would be gate money (at present the $2.50 ground ticket for the CNE guarantees free admission to the snooker) and an opportunity to sell a prestigious event to a sponsor outside the game, particularly if television could again be involved.

This would relieve the pressure on the triple pillars of the Canadian trade, Terry Haddock (Mister Billiard), the promoter, Al and Betty Selinger, (Dufferin Cue) and Mike Holubik (World of Billiards), the co-sponsors, whose generous support is in any event impossible to justify in commercial terms.

The tournament could be telescoped into seven or eight days instead of its present unwieldy three weeks with qualifying competitons held elsewhere before the main event. In this way, much of the present income from entry fees could be maintained.

Companies inside or outside the billiard trade could be encouraged to hire special boxes or tables at the snooker to entertain clients or friends and the press might be persuaded along by promise of liquid refreshments and congenial working conditions. It is not impossible that certain journalists might then discern snooker's potential in terms of regular coverage.

As world champion, Cliff was in a situation of an altogether larger dimension than he had been in before and he did not really have the right kind of professional help he needed to cope with the additional pressures. All he could do was to try his best as a player and he did win the tournament but the result was the only satisfactory thing about it. Snooker Scene's report was as follows.

Cliff Thorburn won his third successive Canadian Open and his fourth in all by beating Terry Griffiths 17–10 in a repeat of last year's final. His capture of the $9,000 first prize, although a triumph of determination, did not reveal him at his best. Like many a world champion before him, he has discovered that there are suddenly dozens of new claims on his attention.

A television documentary team dogged his footsteps, not intrusively but enough to constitute another commitment; there was, as world champion, extra pressure to win before his home crowd; playing conditions from the brain-numbing all-day noise to the oppressively sticky atmosphere, drained mental and physical stamina; and, on top of everything, he had cue trouble.

Now contracted to Adam Custom Cues, Thorburn had not yet adjusted to playing with one. Halfway through the first session of his quarter final against Mario Morra, 25, to whom he at one time trailed 4–5, he changed back to the Dufferin cue with which he won the world championship. Morra, who had seen off an out-of-touch Jim Wych 9–3 is fiercely dedicated but lacks fluency. When he found that he had a real chance of victory, he tried to make too sure of his chances. Each shot, in his own mind, seemed to become a pressure shot and his tempo of play, naturally slow, lost all semblance of continuity as Thorburn peeled off five frames in a row for 9–5.

Tip trouble was Thorburn's next bugbear. His solution was to practise until 4 a.m. for his semi-final with Kirk Stevens, who characteristically attacked him at the start to lead 2–0 and 3–1. Once the match settled down, though, Stevens found inspiration the harder to come by the longer Thorburn kept him out. It was 7–3 before Stevens won another frame as Thorburn closed out the match at 9–5.

The first day of the final was a travesty of top class snooker. CBC's lighting engineers, unfamiliar with snooker's television requirements, arrived at the crack of dawn to rig the lighting necessary for the television coverage on the second day and long before the arrival of the players, had departed. The players needed only the most cursory inspection to realise the worst. Dazzling highlights were reflecting from the tops of the balls and there were deep shadows behind them and, it appeared, almost everywhere. If the referee stood too close this too threw a shadow. It was a Saturday and the engineers could not be recalled.

It was a situation in which Griffiths's patience had much the shorter fuse. Thorburn, of course, was playing under the selfsame lights but was temperamentally better able to adapt to the unfortunate situation. Griffiths does not have a great record of muddling his way through in poor conditions or when playing badly. If he cannot win in style or at least play in a manner in which he can display his ability, he tends to lose interest. Thorburn,

81

whose long apprenticeship of playing for money has moulded his attitudes differently, simply ploughed on oblivious to the match's innumerable mistakes. "I used to worry how I won but I don't any more," he said.

In the 1979 final, Thorburn led Griffiths 10–3 but scraped home only 17–16. This time he led 13–3 overnight. With the lights reset for the second day's play, Griffiths gave some indication of what the final could have been by winning six frames out of eight in an afternoon session highlighted by his break of 121 but there was never any real prospect that he could close the ten-frame gap with which he had started the day.

This was the last time the Canadian Open was staged at the Canadian National Exhibition Centre. The British circuit was starting to expand so tournament dates were in shorter supply. The new British events were also carrying prize money of a level far in excess of what Canada could offer so the inexorable laws of supply and demand brought about the demise of the tournament.

Meanwhile, Cliff came over to England to move into his new house at Walton-on-Thames, about ten days before the Champion of Champions tournament at the New London Theatre, a promotional disaster of rare magnitude. With neither television coverage nor sponsorship materialising, the event lost an estimated £30,000 and when Doug Mountjoy beat John Virgo 10–8 in the final his winner's envelope contained no cheque.

There were two round robin groups with the winner of each going into the final. Cliff lost 8–1 to Terry Griffiths, 5–4 to Alex Higgins, 8–1 to Doug Mountjoy and beat Graham Miles 5–4. It was not the way he would have chosen to make his first appearance in Britain as world champion. "My attitude wasn't right," was all he said at the time but serious problems were already emerging.

The Canadian Open at the Canadian National Exhibition Centre 1980. To my immediate right Al Selinger, to my immediate left, his wife Betty. Together they run Dufferin Cue. Left of Al is Mike Holubik and right of Betty is Terry Haddock. But for these four people, nothing much would have happened on the Canadian scene around this time.

I'd said that I had to move over here to win the championship. And I'd won the championship without moving over here. So now I moved over here. I'd somehow put myself in the position of having to do something I didn't really want to do. About four days after we'd moved into the house, we're stood by the front door and I'm off to play a show and I said to Barb: "What the hell have we done here?" I'd have been quite happy to group some exhibitions or tournaments together, go home for a rest and then come back, but now I've moved here.

Del Simmons was taking my bookings at the time. He said that I would be quite busy and I said that I didn't want to work all the time. He said: "You've got to do it. This is your big year. You might never win it again."

And I thought: "Jesus Christ, who wants to think about that?" So I said that I'd like to charge more than Alex so I wouldn't get so much work.

He said: "You can't do that".

I said: "Why not?"

"You just can't."

I started to get a little bit discouraged, driving and playing all over the place. I was discouraged also that I couldn't charge more than Alex. It was myself against Del and Alex it seemed. I couldn't control this situation and I was very disappointed.

I really didn't have much help then. I was over here by myself with Barb. I was stuck out at Walton-on-Thames and I'd go down to Kingston Snooker Centre with John Virgo, Jimmy White and guys like that. So I'm just one of the boys. I'd have been better off living up in Keswick. I came from a place where I was a little fish in a big pond. Maybe I needed a small pond up in Keswick. Now that I'm involved with Robert (Winsor), it's good to have someone to say: "You're the best, you can do it." I've been doing things on my own ever since I left home, ever since I started playing snooker, but it is easier sometimes if you've the right kind of help.

Then my cue went. I had to try to play with it because I hadn't got time to find another and get used to it. Even at the Champion of Champions I was sticking bits of paper in the joint but of course it would soon work loose.

In about a year I must have played 30 or 40 shows with Alex and even though I was world champion he always got twice as big an ovation as I did. I could understand this in a way but it still gets through to you. I always think it's funny when Alex says that he's travelling so much that he can't practise properly. It doesn't seem to have occurred to him that he doesn't have to play.

Kirk, Bill and I then played in the second World Cup, also at the New London Theatre where we beat England 8–5 in the semi-finals. The three top English players of that time were Fred Davis, David Taylor and John Virgo. The only thing I can remember about the match is Bill splitting his trousers when he was playing David and we were leading 6–4. This was not a small split but the whole back seam.

What was worse, Bill doesn't wear any underwear. Normally, Bill has a very wide stance but when he was shooting a blue into the middle pocket I could see he was standing all wrong with his feet together, trying to squeeze his cheeks together. We had to call a time-out and find someone with needle and thread to stitch his trousers back up. After about 15 minutes Bill came back to the arena to a huge cheer. I see that I was quoted at the time as saying: "This is really a needle match. I was hoping that Bill was going to sew it up for us."

Next day, we lost 8–5 to Wales in the final after the start had been delayed 35 minutes. Kirk and I were caught in a traffic jam caused by an anti-nuclear weapons demonstration. There we were in Regents Park, stuck in the middle of 40,000 people. I asked this cop to help us and he said: "Well, I guess you've just been snookered, Cliff." He thought this was funnier than I did. We left the car and jumped on a tube from Sloane Square. Two hundred yards from the venue, Kirk took his suit and cue, left me with everything else and ran the rest of the way.

Kirk was living with Barb and me at the time but, looking back on it, this wasn't such a good idea. I didn't know him all that well but I wanted him to have a different situation to what I had had when I first came over. In those days, I didn't know anybody and I thought why should Kirk go through what I had to go through. The game in 1980 was also much better than it was in 1973. The money was starting to be quite good and exhibitions were £200 or £300 a night. I felt I'd like to give Kirk a good chance and Barb would feed him and do his laundry and all that. We had some good times, but there were others when I wanted to wring his neck and he seemed to me a little bit lazy in terms of making the most of the opportunities he had.

Once, I'd played in Newcastle and drove back that night. I got in about 4.30. The doorbell rings at five after eight: "Taxi for Mr Stevens. He has to get the nine o'clock plane to Leeds." I go upstairs. Kirk's asleep and I'm trying to wake him. It's at least 30 minutes to the airport. At 8.15 he's still in bed. I finally get him out and he says: "OK but I need a bath".

Why should I have pressure in this situation? What's it to do with me? Anyway, he has his bath and now it's 8.30. He comes downstairs. I'm fuming and I'm just wanting him to go. Then he says: "Just let me have a bowl of cereal." I want to strangle him but he has his bowl of cereal and somehow he gets to the airport and catches the plane, which was ten minutes late or something. That started to happen a lot. Kirk would say: "I don't feel like playing" and things like that. I used to feel the same when things were going badly but this boy had no other means of making any money. In that situation you just have to get out and do it.

Over the next few years he still did pretty well overall and got up to fourth in the rankings but it was all so good for him that he just never looked to the next year. Now, saying this in 1987, it looks as if next year might not be there in the sense of making some real money. That's when the self-doubt really gets to creep in and he's really going to have to get hold of himself to climb back up. Kirk has to be coaxed but he also has to have a strict guiding hand behind him. I felt like Kirk's my kid brother in a way, but he wouldn't actually let anybody get that close to him.

In November, Steve Davis won the Coral UK Championship at Preston. Overseas players were still barred from this event, except for Bill Werbeniuk whose entry was accepted because he was then established as a British resident. Davis powered through the field before slaughtering Higgins in the final 16–6. It was the start of a two-year period in which, with rare exceptions, he looked almost unbeatable, even if over-confidence was his undoing in the Benson and Hedges Masters debut in January 1981 when he lost 5–3 to Perrie Mans.

Cliff then beat Mans 5–4 in a 4½ hour battle, potting a good pink and black to make it 4–4 and winning the decider with a break of 84. A cruel disappointment was to follow, all the more cruel because Higgins was involved. Cliff led him 5–1 in their semi-final but Higgins won 6–5. Here is *Snooker Scene*'s report of the match.

Alex Higgins 6 Cliff Thorburn 5

Scores: 37–79; 82(49)–22; 34–100(70); 28–74(42); 22–69(30,35); 71–30; 79(40)–5; 85(85)–57; 61–52(38); 83(77)–35(30)

Ashen-faced when he arrived for the match, Higgins revealed that he had "thrown up five or six times" that morning. He attributed his upset stomach to "some West Country mustard" he had put on a steak the previous night. Subdued and off colour, he trailed 1–4 at the half-hour mid-session interval, during which he actually dozed off for ten minutes.

Thorburn having played very efficiently thus far, only one result seemed conceivable, all the more so when the Canadian went to 5–1. On a lesser occasion, in front of a smaller crowd, Higgins might have succumbed relatively quietly and even when he summoned a couple of defiant flourishes to win the next two frames, Thorburn did not look in any danger.

At 5–3, 57–0, Thorburn seemed about to cross the finish line. With some justification, he was angered by newspaper reports that he then missed a simple red, although it was not obvious, either from a television monitor or most seats in the arena itself, that another ball was partially obscuring the red he attempted. In his quiet, undemonstrative way Thorburn did not telegraph that the shot involved any significant degree of difficulty as some players might have done! Whatever the degree of difficulty was, Higgins interpreted the Canadian's failure as a reprieve and sprang to life with a scintillating winning clearance of 85.

It was clear that the balance of the match had changed. Experienced Thorburn-watchers recalled that he had lost from four in front with five to play against Eddie Charlton in the 1978 world quarter-finals and indeed had either had difficulty in clinching or failing to clinch winning positions in numerous big matches. Thorburn repudiated the suggestion that this aspect of his previous history had any bearing on the match in hand but two shots in particular appeared to counter this view . . .

A good long red enabled him to embark on a 38 break which took him to 52–17 in the tenth. In potting a red, he opened a cluster but, covering himself on the black, had to take the pink in the middle, a shot which he would ordinarily get but which this time he missed. His vital mistake in this frame, though, was the last red which, at 52–34, he attempted along the cushion into a baulk pocket. The pot was risky, safety a legitimate option. Played more firmly, the red might have wobbled clear of the pocket. As it was, Thorburn did not go through with his shot. The red was never on target and only dribbled tamely over the pocket. Higgins took the frame on the pink.

Thorburn again played a couple of good shots at the start of the decider but, with his lead having built up to 35–6, missed a black from its spot, a fatal mistake as it proved. Higgins attempted a long red into one baulk pocket, fluked it in the other and unstoppably ran 77 to reach his fourth consecutive Masters final. "Cliff didn't lose that match. Alex won it. Alex is the only player who could have won it from that position," said Kirk Stevens.

Three factors – a reprieve, a big crowd getting right behind him and in the last frame, the kind of fluke which seems to convince him that the gods are on his side – combined to unlock Higgins's ability and produce his magnificent charge, but Thorburn would still have won if he had not, excusably perhaps, cracked a little in the last couple of frames.

Few matches – and certainly not this one – are wholly won or wholly lost. The less romantic but more sober truth is that a variable combination of mistakes and good play determines results and the attempt to unravel why one shot is missed rather than another remains one of snooker's endless fascinations.

Thorburn shook Higgins by the hand with his customary good grace, but defeat in such circumstances must have been galling indeed. He badly needed to win a tournament in Britain to remind the British public that he is world champion, for he had received only a fraction of the recognition and acclam that Terry Griffiths, for instance, received from winning the title and that Higgins invariably receives, win or lose. Instead of re-affirming his status as No 1, the match merely re-activated memories, probably with him and certainly with his many admirers, of matches that he has lost when he should have won.

Nothing seemed to be going right. Even when Cliff won the Lada Classic, then only a four-man invitation tournament in Newcastle, he may have felt that he was not receiving full credit because Snooker Scene described his semi-final with Terry Griffiths as "most unsatisfactory". This was because the first cue ball was discarded after an extraordinary number of kicks and the second because it was discovered to be under size. In the Benson and Hedges Irish Masters he beat Doug Mountjoy 4–0 and led Terry Griffiths 5–4 only for Griffiths to win the last two frames with breaks of 93 and 91. His year as champion was drawing to a close. He had earned scarcely a bean other than prize money and exhibition fees. He had made the wrong decision to live in England. His confidence had been eroded. Even so, he had his game in reasonable shape by the time it came for his title defence in Sheffield. After beating Graham Miles 13–2 and David Taylor 13–6 he played Steve Davis in the semi-finals.

It made it very hard to play to have Steve's crowd from Romford all there. They had this flag draped over the balcony, there was always a terrific cheer when he came into the arena and there was a lot of applause for anything of his that looked like a good shot. I could have coped with all this but what blew my mind in the third session was a whistling which came from the balcony when I was about to play. I stopped. The whistles started again. I stopped again. Steve won that game to make it 10–10. Steve must have heard the whistling, but didn't do anything to stop it so at the end of the session I did something I very much regret.

Steve had irritated me some more by coming across to shake hands when the pink and black were still on the table in the last frame of the day. I needed eight snookers but this was not the point. It was up to me to concede when I was ready. I indicated that I was going to play on and went to address the cue ball. I imitated Steve's habit of stepping away from the table to take a sip of water, addressed the cue ball again and then, without striking it, walked across to him to offer my handshake.

When we got backstage, I said: "You're an arrogant bastard Davis. I'll be looking for you tomorrow."

When I'd cooled down I felt bad about what I had done and I apologised on television next day. What never came out at the time, though, was the provocation that I'd had with this whistling from the balcony. John Carty, who was editor of the *Cue World* at the time, was on that balcony and told me about two years later: "That was really disgusting what they did to you". I asked him why he hadn't written this at the time because the public might then have understood that the fault was not all on one side.

I was 12–10 down overnight and the next day I just hadn't got it. Steve beat me 16–10 and then beat Doug Mountjoy 18–12 in the final.

Steve Davis 16 Cliff Thorburn 10

Scores – Session 1: 22–92(49); 79(45)–41; 62–43(32); 85(51)–26; 45(38)–73; 11–71; 66(31, 30)–54(54); (Davis 4–3). Session 2: 53–1; 34–56; 52–38; 0–67; 4–123(91); 6–79(47); 25–78(31); (Thorburn 8–6). Session 3: 61–46; 77(47)–40(32); 56–67(37); 59(34)–46; 111(59,40)–15; 57–46(37); 42–81; 80(32)–23; (Davis 12–10). Session 4: 65(44)–42(30); 96(50)–22; 82(41)–39; 60–49

Winning the last frame of a 3hr 34 min opening session from 0–54, Davis led 4–3 at the first interval. Next morning, the first three frames occupied 2hr 11 min. When Davis won two of them to lead 6–4 it seemed that Thorburn's style and tactical policy were cutting little ice. Suddenly, the Canadian broke through, producing a deadly combination of Scrooge-like safety play and meticulous breakbuilding to which there was no apparent answer.

For an hour, Davis did not pot a ball. In three frames, he potted only three. At 7–6, 54–0 Thorburn made his first mistake for 3½ frames but Davis, his rhythm and concentration blown to pieces, missed the half-chance to recover that he might well have accepted in a faster flowing game.

The idea of championship snooker is to undermine your opponent's confidence and self-control. Higgins attempts it with his speed and a highly individual style which gets crowds behind him. Davis with a textbook technique which makes snooker look a matter of simple mechanics. Thorburn with a freezing out technique. Every method is useless, of course, unless the player concerned is also potting the balls when he has the opportunity, though his demeanour when he is not is also important. Davis can usually convey the impression, either by a smile or other facial expressiveness that a mistake is a momentary lapse rather than a sign of weakness.

In the second session, the mask slipped and Davis looked almost broken as he sat in his corner, closing his eyes for half a minute at a time as he tried to clear his mind and motivate himself anew. It was therefore extraordinary that Davis, after an afternoon's rest, should front up so apparently bright and fresh to receive his customary full-throated reception from his supporters at the start of the evening session.

Crucially, Davis won two arduous frames of 35 and 34 minutes to level at 8–8. One of 60 minutes put Thorburn back in front at 9–8 and one of 29 brought the Londoner again at 9–9. Each of these four bitterly contested frames depended on the last few colours. They were all played very tightly with much safety and for the most part fragmentary scoring but, differently from the morning session, Thorburn was unable to obtain a psychological ascendancy.

Those who believed that Davis was fated to win the championship pointed to the conclusion of the 20th frame as evidence. Leading 10–9, Davis three times attempted black for game. Once it went safe; once it offered a very difficult chance for Thorburn, once a slightly easier chance into a middle pocket. Davis refused a fourth chance in favour of safety and forced the error from which he went to 11–9.

Resuming at 12–10, Davis was blessed with the smile which fortune so often bestows on the man in form. As he potted the brown which guaranteed him (barring snookers) 13–10, the cue ball rolled perilously near the middle pocket. Had it dropped in instead of catching the jaw and staying out, Thorburn would surely not have missed brown from its spot and the sitting blue, pink and black which would not only have narrowed the gap to one frame but give the Canadian a new infusion of hope.

Those who had not seen BBC's preview of the championship may well have been mystified, as referee Len Ganley clearly was, by Davis's insistence, before breaking off in the following frame, that the balls be reracked. Davis had recalled how in the Tolly Cobbold Classic two years previously Ray Reardon had had the balls reracked "four or five times" and expressed himself certain that this had been done "to get him at it". How far these two incidents were consciously or subconsciously connected in his mind only Davis can say.

From Davis's break off, Thorburn went in-off attempting a long red. Davis made 50, playing one shot left handed bridging over a ball, and from that point it was difficult to envisage him losing. It is never easy against Thorburn but the Canadian could not, it seemed, pot the balls that really mattered in the final session. The four frames that morning took 2hrs 32 min but Davis won them all.

So I wasn't still champion when I went to the Guinness Festival of Snooker in a holiday camp on the Isle of Wight. It rained all week and I was scratched from the main event in the last 16. I had just beaten John Campbell 4–3, giving him 25 start, which wasn't bad because he'd won the Australian amateur championship a couple of times and was ready to turn professional, and went back to my room to rest for

The finalists in the what was billed as the world mixed doubles championships in the Guinness Festival of Snooker on the Isle of Wight in 1981. John Virgo played with Vera Selby and Natalie Stelmach, who was then the best of the Canadian girls, played with me

my next match. The time for it was altered, I went on watching television and the match was awarded to my opponent, Alf Micallef, a Maltese who was then living, I'm told, in Portsmouth. There were protests and even a suggestion that all the professionals would walk out but, in the end, the decision stood and I was scratched.

I did manage to win what was billed as the world mixed doubles championship with Natalie Stelmach, who was then the best of the Canadian girls, but it wasn't much consolation.

A lot of the trouble was my cue. I was fed up with the one I had won the championship with and I was dabbling with two or three others, but always going back to old faithful, except that it wasn't very old and it wasn't very faithful. The problem with my cue was in the metal joint. If a little sliver of metal comes off it, it starts to self-destruct. I kept trying to patch it up but it was no good and I should have got rid of it a long time before I did.

Finally, I was forced into doing something by what happened in a tournament in Malta. There were two three-man groups with two to go forward from each to the semi-finals. I beat Joe Grech, one of Malta's two good amateurs at the time, 5–2. Grech then beat Higgins 4–3 so I only had to win one frame against Higgins to get into the semi-finals. I lost 7–0. That did it. I realised that the only way I could get rid of the cue was to sell it to someone I would never see again. Then I would have to concentrate on one of the other cues. Maybe it should have gone into the Sports Hall of Fame in Canada but I had visions of breaking into the place late at night and hacking the glass open so that I could get it back.

I sold it to a guy for £50. He wasn't quite sure that I was telling the truth that it really was the cue I'd won the world championship with. We did the deal on a parking lot. It was like something out of a Mafia type movie – maybe the *Maltese Falcon* – as if we were out there buying and selling contraband. We had to put the lights on the car so that we would see the money being passed and that the guy was getting the right cue.

I felt better once I'd got rid of the cue, but I still had some problems before I finally settled with the one I have now. It's virtually impossible to get two pieces of wood the same. Cues are not machine-made like golf clubs. All that you can do is build your game around the cue.

This was the year I won Pot Black but I never really enjoyed playing in it. The matches were only one frame. There was a lot of hanging about at the BBC in Birmingham between Christmas and the New Year and the atmosphere in the studio never felt right for a snooker match. June Davis, Joe's widow, is on the left, having just presented me with the trophy. George Howard, who was then director general of the BBC, is on my other side talking to Jim Wych. Going along the line to the right are Eddie Charlton, Kirk Stevens, Ray Reardon, Alex Higgins, John Williams (the referee), Steve Davis, David Taylor, Ted Lowe (commentator) and Alan Weeks (compère)

SEVEN

THE DOWN SIDE

IF I THOUGHT that the 1980–81 season had been a disaster, it came to look like a golden age in comparison with 1981–82. Jamie was born in July 1981 and only he and Barb got me through the season. I didn't seem to have any perspective and I couldn't seem to get the values of the situation in the right order. I was in total disarray and but for Barb and Jamie I could just have packed up and not come back to Britain for a couple of years.

Jamie was born on July 17, 1981. He was supposed to be born two weeks later so that day I was looking forward to a day out at the British Open. I had got to know Sam Torrance and he was playing at Royal St George's at 9.30 so I'm going to get up at 5 o'clock, have a nice shower and drive down to his hotel. I'm going to meet some of Sam's friends, have a champagne breakfast and follow them round.

At 4.30 I feel this tap, tap, on my shoulder.

"Honey, I think I've broken my water."

And for about 30 seconds I'm thinking: "No, Barb. Not today. Don't do this to me."

This might have been selfishness or panic or both but anyway it's only lasted a few seconds. Barb already has her bag packed. I'm tuned in to what is really happening and I'm driving her to the hospital.

Jamie was born about ten hours later. Sam shot 66.

There was a new tournament to start the season, the Langs Scottish Masters. It's developed into a good event now but there was some teething troubles in the first year, one of which was that we played at the Kelvin Hall, which holds well over 2,000 people. I think there was only one session when it was even half-full. I beat Kirk 5–1 and then I had another run-in with Higgins. It was two-all and Alex needed snookers in the fifth. Then he said the score was wrong – which it turned out

Sam Torrance and I enjoy a round of golf on a typical British summer's day

it was – although it made no real difference. Alex knows the rules: you're taken to have condoned any mistake if you play on, which he had. There was no check scorer and the referee had called the score wrong but that was not the point. Alex made a big fuss, called me a cheat when it was over and tried to talk the organisers into playing the match over again.

I went upstairs to my hotel room. The phone rang. Higgins said: "I hope to hell your son doesn't grow up to be like you". Jamie was then less than three months old. I slammed the phone down, charged out of the door and pushed the button on the lift. I would have thrown Alex all over his room. The lift opened up and two people came out who wanted to chat. I cooled off and let it go.

It didn't do me any good for the final, though. I was leading Jimmy White 4–1 and I lost eight in a row. Alex sat in Jimmy's manager's box, right in the front row. After the match, there was an auction for a football which had been used in one of Celtic's matches or something and Alex bought it for £75. He got up and said: "I'd like to give this to Jimmy because he really deserves it". What was he trying to do to me?

Things just went from bad to worse. I lost 5–0 to Graham Miles in the first Jameson International at Romiley Forum, Stockport. This was bad enough, but then I was told that I had to go out to play an exhibition frame to give the spectators value for their tickets. I didn't want to but eventually I played. I made a good red and doubled the black. A voice came out from near the back: "Why couldn't you do it when it counted?"

I said: "I don't need this," and just walked out. I was having a lot of trouble with this cue and the one good thing about the whole incident was that I was so mad that I just broke it across my knee in the dressing room, just snapped it. Having done that, I had to look for a new one instead of just trying a new one and then going back to the one I was using.

I lost again to Jimmy White in the Northern Ireland Classic in Belfast 5–2; we lost to England in the semi-finals of the World Cup, and I lost to Tony Meo 9–6 in the Coral UK, which I was allowed to play in for the first time because I was considered a UK resident. I lost 5–1 to Terry Griffiths in the Lada Classic, the one that Steve made the first televised maximum in. I practised hard for the Benson and Hedges Masters and the morning of my first match I made a 141 and a 138 back to back at Kingston Snooker Centre. I drove from there to the venue and got caught in a traffic jam. I got to Wembley with five minutes to spare. It had taken me an hour and threequarters altogether for a journey that was 40 minutes top. I lost 5–0 to Tony Meo.

At the Benson and Hedges Irish Masters I led Higgins 4–0 and lost 5–4. I just couldn't beat him for some reason. I was hating him and feeling sorry for him at the same time. I feel better now that I just can't stand the guy and don't feel sorry for him any more. Later that week I was in the bar and Higgins was playing cards. I just happened to be sat beside the girl who was with him on the night. Higgins has been drinking and suddenly says: "Thorburn you're a Canadian cunt and you can't fucking play either". This was too much. He walked over to me and I'm so mad I just hit him. Not quite on the chin, more like his jaw to the side. He's gone down. Some of his friends grabbed him; some other people grabbed me. Some drunk says: "Let's all be friends." Actually he says it two or three times. So eventually, as we go to shake hands, I kick him right in the nuts.

I didn't even feel like playing in the world championship and lost 10–4 to Jimmy White. I lost the first six frames.

Barb and I had been back home in January and February to look at some houses. We'd made up our minds to move back to Canada. We looked at about 30 homes and bought the one which was the first that we'd looked at. I don't do things easily. Even then I was grinding. It was like my shot selection. I know what I'm going to do right away but I double-check. After the 1982 championship we went back. Our stuff was shipped home in June.

Cliff had sunk so low that he could only go upwards. Periodically, a player needs to lose control to gain control; to stop trying so that he can try harder after a respite from his efforts. Snooker had changed so dramatically from what it had been only five years previously that it was no longer feasible for leading players to accept almost everything that was offered. In this respect, the world title often became a poisoned chalice even if it took almost a year for the poisons from all the stresses of being champion to work through the system.

Terry Griffiths, world champion in 1979, lost 13–10 in the first round to Steve Davis in 1980 after trailing 0–7. Cliff, the 1980 champion, had buckled under another set of stresses and pressures. Davis, the 1981 champion, was so mentally and physically exhausted from playing or just appearing here and everywhere that he lost 10–1 in the first round to Tony Knowles in 1982, the year when Alex Higgins won his second world title. A similar phenomenon was manifest a little later as the games of Dennis Taylor, the 1985 world champion, and Joe Johnson, the 1986 world champion, who both, later or sooner, fell apart during their years as title-holder.

Rest, reappraisal, refreshment of spirit and, where appropriate, a new start is often what is called for and for the whole of the summer of 1982 Cliff concentrated on his golf, getting down to a five handicap and taking the relaxation he needed. He had returned home in the summer of 1981, chiefly to visit his and Barbara's parents but in the way of many a parental visit this tended to add to rather than reduce stress. In implementing his important decision to move back to Canada, he had made one element of a new start. He also needed to find and persevere with a new cue.

From 1976 to 1982, I'd always had cues custom-made, but I got to the point where I didn't like the way the cue actually felt. So this time I just picked one up that felt good and started to play with it once a week through the summer. I sanded it down here and there to give it the kind of taper that I like. It started to feel good and it is still the cue I play with now.

My first tournament was the Jameson International. I beat George Scott 5–1, which was the first match that I'd won for a year, and lost 5–2 to Dennis Taylor after winning the first two frames. I wasn't playing that much better than I had been the previous season but I did feel like playing again and felt that I could win if I didn't go for too many shots and just kept concentrating.

I lost 5–2 to Bill Werbeniuk in the Professional Players Tournament, which has now become the Rothmans. The match was at Sutton Coldfield and I had to drive over from Chesterfield for a 10.30 start. I got in a massive traffic jam and arrived ten minutes late. The referee said that he would dock me a frame, but Bill said that if he did that he would lose the next game on purpose. It was a pretty classy move on Bill's part but he is like that. He wanted to beat me level and he thought that he could at the time. He played well and at that time I could only play well for a game or two before I lost my concentration.

The first sign I had that I was on the way back was when Bill, Kirk and I won the State Express World Cup at Reading. We beat England 4–2 in the final. Bill beat Steve Davis 2–1 in the afternoon and I beat Steve 2–0 to clinch it.

Steve had been quoted in the papers as saying that I couldn't handle success. I'm not quite sure what he meant by that. Who can? You always go wrong somewhere. Steve's proved that. He also said that he didn't like the way that I played – which is tough on him.

I was very glad that I won that particular match because it certainly stopped Steve saying things like that afterwards. It was to everybody's benefit, I think, because Steve was maybe getting a bit carried away at that time. Or maybe Barry Hearn was getting carried away on his behalf.

Bill was quoted afterwards in *Snooker Scene*: "This has proved that there are no superstars in snooker, just a hell of a lot of real good players". The press and television were making celebrities out of Steve, Jimmy White and Tony Knowles and, as Bill said: "Steve, Jimmy and Tony are all very good players and on top of that they are young and good looking. Jimmy and Tony are both exceptionally quick and play a very open kind of game which the public likes to see. That's OK but I think that Joe Public can be blinded sometimes by the glamour that has been put round these players. I think it's good for the public to realise that there is more than one way to play this game well.

"What I'm really hoping is that the BBC will sell the tape of us winning to the Canadian networks back home because snooker needs it there. Even when Cliff won the world championship in 1980, the media interest didn't amount to much and didn't last very long. When you compare how little attention Cliff had when he was world champion and the publicity machine which got behind Steve when he won in 1981 you would have to feel disappointed by the lack of recognition. As a matter of fact, I think the world team title will be more important back home because a team is more representative of a country than an individual. That's how they'll look at it anyway.

"Snooker in Canada still has the image of guys playing for each other's money in some pool hall. No one there seems to grasp just how well it is presented in Britain, but if they see the tape of the State Express maybe it will help someone get a big televised sponsored tournament together. Canadian snooker needs it and the game needs it as part of the overseas circuit which has to develop to support what we have in Britain."

These were good words of Bill's. The only trouble was, nothing came of them.

There was yet another change of regulation for the Coral UK. This year, all overseas players were banned so I next played in the Hofmeister World Doubles with John Virgo. We lost 6–2 in the quarter-finals to Steve Davis and Tony Meo. We played at Crystal Palace, which was cold and completely unsuitable for snooker, and the tournament has been altogether much better since it's been played at the Derngate Centre, Northampton.

The Lada Classic was extended from eight to 16 players and given full ITV network coverage. Cliff Wilson and I gave them a problem by finishing the first four frames in an hour. They weren't prepared for this as they had nothing to fill the interval so we played seven frames before we came off. I won 5–3 so obviously we only played one frame after the interval. This wouldn't be tolerated these days as it is important for the players to know when the mid-session interval is going to be taken. If one player is playing well, he naturally wants to play on, particularly if the other player is struggling. It can be very unfair on one player to have an unscheduled break.

Kirk beat me in the quarter-finals, 5–3. Someone asked me at the press conference whether it was true that he was only 12 years old when I first played him. I said that it was but that he had improved a lot since he was 12. I thought that Kirk would win the tournament, but he lost to Bill in the semi-finals and Bill was 5–5 with Steve in the final before he lost 9–5. It was easy to see why we'd won the world team. Bill was playing the best snooker he's ever played in Britain. Kirk had just beaten me and I wasn't playing so badly either.

Three weeks later, I won the Benson and Hedges Masters, which is an event I've always loved. It's in London. It's played in a big arena, it's well organised, it has class. I said in my victory speech: "This is the Big Daddy after the world championship".

In my first match against Joe Johnson I lost two of the first three frames and was 40 behind in the next. I was 0–55 in the sixth and won this as well. I won 5–2, but this was not the easiest 5–2 I've had. The quarter-final against Terry Griffiths was a turning point for me. It was 3–3 and I needed two reds, two blacks and all the colours to win the seventh. It was one of the best clearances I've ever made. I knew I was back from that clearance alone. I won 5–3.

It took me six hours and 12 minutes to beat Eddie Charlton 6–5 in the semi-finals. Unknown to me, there was a backstage sweep on what time we would finish and some of the entrants saw the times they'd chosen pass before we'd even reached the interval. I didn't care how long it took, particularly as I wasn't the only one playing safe. Eddie was two up with three to play so it was very satisfying to turn it round from the time he beat me from four down with five to play in the 1978 world quarter-finals.

In the final, I played Ray Reardon, who was having a good season. He'd beaten Jimmy White to win the PPT and after the Masters he won the Welsh championship and beat Jimmy again in the final of the Yamaha Trophy, which I didn't play in because I didn't like the short match round robin format for the early rounds. When I was leading 7–4, I made a 69 clearance to win the next frame after Ray had led 68–0. This put me four up with five to play but we then had a half-hour interval, which is far too long, however much chance you want to give the crowd to get a drink. I see that I said at the time: "It's too long. If you think a lot, as I do, you can get totally confused." Maybe the reason so many matches are won by the player who's behind at the interval is something to do with this.

It seemed to do something for Ray, though, because he made a 65 and 113 in the next two frames and then made it 7–8. My attitude was more mature in this kind of situation than it had been in the past. Once you've lost the last four or five in a row a few times to lose the match, you start to think why you've lost. Looking back, I had maybe tried to lock it up too much instead of going for balls as you should when you're three or four frames in front. Anyway, I managed just to concentrate and just play the balls in the next frame and when I got in close I made 56 to clinch it. I was back.

Just a few times in my life, I've felt as good as a snooker player can possibly feel. In the last frame against Higgins in the 1980 final, I was so numb I didn't feel any pressure. I seemed to be very tall, very high as I looked at the table. I could work everything out without thinking. I was thinking as positively as anyone could possibly think except that I didn't seem to be thinking at all.

This was how I felt when I made my 147 against Terry Griffiths in the second round of the 1983 world championship. There was not the slightest shake or tremor in my whole body. I was rock solid. In fact, I felt nearly as good as this the whole of the 1983 world tournament except by the final I was so mentally exhausted that I knew I couldn't beat Steve.

I'd also got my business affairs into shape. Mike Watterson, who still promoted the world championship and several other major tournaments in those days, was managing me in Britain while Darryl McKerrow had just started to do a few things for me in Canada. I had felt with Q Promotions, which was run by Maurice Hayes, and with ISA, which was Del Simmons, that I was just a statistic, a name they could put in their advertising to add to the credibility of whoever happened to be managing Higgins. They would throw me the odd bone when I started barking too much. I guess at the time I didn't have a lot of choice because there weren't many snooker managements about. The only alternative was to do my own bookings and sort out my own tax and I didn't want to do that.

Del came up with a company called Sports Stars Isle of Man, the idea being that this would be a way of not paying so much tax, but with all the aggravation it gave me I was better off not doing anything. I was getting bills that weren't even itemised and I was even offered a chance to put my money through Cyprus. The people who were advising me at the time, friends of Del's, said it was good for me and really easy but I thought that one day they might call the soldiers back in there and there I would be at this bank in Cyprus with my cue trying to get my money out with everybody shooting all around me. Kirk had also got himself into a bit of a jam so he was with Mike, too.

The great thing about it when Mike was managing me was that I stayed at his cottage. There was a snooker table about 15 feet away from my bed. Kirk, Jim Wych and I all practised together for two weeks on Mike's table, which was just like the tables we were using in the world championship, and it certainly helped get our games into shape. None of us could meet before the quarter-finals so we were each for each other in a way, saying the odd thing to help, and talking snooker. This was much better than having to go to a snooker club by myself and motivate myself.

I beat John Campbell in the first round at the Crucible, 10–5. I'd known him since I'd beaten him for some money put up by his backer in Brisbane in 1980. I knew that he'd been improving all the time on what we'd seen then and when we were 5–5 I was thinking: "This guy's a pretty good player".

I made the 147 against Terry in the first session. It made it 3–1 and I was glad it was the mid-session interval then because I needed some time to get over it. I had seen myself winning the championship long before I knew even what the trophy looked like and I could see myself holding it up. I visualised the 147 as well but not how I would act after I'd done it. I have always visualised – or is it fantasised – in the same way. I've done it with golf ever since I first played. It can be 8.30 at night and the sun can be down behind the trees but in my mind, as I hit my five iron up towards the green, there are 20,000 people in the stands and I need a birdie to win the Masters.

The champagne is for my 147 maximum in the 1983 world championship

When I'm not playing so well I like to watch the tape of the 147. I always cringe when I stop after potting the 14th red. In fact, I had a slight cold. My nose was running and I could feel this stuff coming down on to my moustache. I could just see myself knocking in the last black and having this stuff all over my face. Looking back, it's obvious that I did think I was going to make the maximum so there was I thinking: "Let's get ready for the big number."

They said afterwards that the yellow was the best shot. All I can say about that is that my mind was in such good shape that I wasn't shooting the yellow after 15 blacks: I was just shooting the yellow. Anyway, I thought the green was the best shot because I had to squeeze the cue ball by the brown to get on the brown.

The yellow made a nice crack as it went in, but the green was even better, dead centre of the pocket. I hit it perfectly. The sound of it just made me feel so good. When I was down on the brown, I was every spectator in the place. I just knew I was going to do it. It was as if I was watching myself. It was the weirdest feeling. I've had it a few times since, even if it hasn't been with anything quite as dramatic as winning the world championship and knocking in the 147. When I potted the last black I was just so relieved and so happy I just dropped to my knees. It brings tears to my eyes every time I watch it.

Nothing else about the match stands out until it was 12–9. Terry won a couple of black ball games and in both I had black for the match but both times I was near the cushion. At 12–11, Terry made a 97 to make it 12–12. Even then I didn't think I was going to lose and I made a 75 in the decider.

After the session when I made the 147 I got to know that Barbara had lost what would have been our second baby. I had gone up to the sponsor's room and sprayed some champagne. One of the photographers suggested that I phone Barb to tell her what had happened so that they could take some pictures of me phoning her. I got through to her, told her that I'd just made a 147 and she said: "That's great". Then she said that she was really sorry because she had lost the baby.

So there were these photographers taking pictures and they're saying: "Smile. Go on what's the matter with you?" Talk about timing. I didn't want people to know that it had happened. I felt that it was private.

I had to win the last three to beat Kirk 13–12 in the quarter-finals. All the world knows about the problems Kirk has had with drug addiction because they were plastered all over the newspapers in 1985. Anybody who had spent much time in pool halls in Canada and North America – other than the ones which are high class – couldn't have avoided coming into contact with drugs and drug users. A lot of young guys sample stuff just for the hell of it then decide it's bad for them and just don't get involved any more. Somehow, Kirk got hooked. I'm not passing any moral judgment on that because he had some things happen to him which anybody would have found agonising to cope with. His mother died in a fire which was started by arson and one of his sisters almost died from drug addiction when her veins burst. I'm certain that Kirk never took anything to improve his performance. He just felt he needed something to get him from day to day. At the world doubles at Crystal Palace a few months earlier, Kirk had ended up in hospital from using some contaminated drugs someone had sold him. I had my suspicions who had sold them to him. When I saw this guy coming out of Kirk's dressing room at the mid-session interval of the first session when it was 4–0, I flipped. I may have been wrong. I'm not suggesting Kirk was on drugs while he was playing but I just felt that if that guy stayed it would affect me too much. I told Mike Watterson and he had him thrown out.

So now I'd won two 13–12s in a row. I was trying not to think too much about Barb losing the baby and once I was into my matches I was concentrating well. No-one in Sheffield knew about it until Terry Haddock of Snooker Canada came over from Toronto in time for the semi-finals and happened to mention it. Of course, he didn't know that no-one in England knew about it yet. This was when I was playing Tony Knowles in the semi-finals and then the press wouldn't stop bugging me about it. In the last frame of the second session, when it was 7–7, I only needed one snooker, but I just couldn't think about the game any more and conceded. I would have lost the game anyway, but I just couldn't sit there in the chair. I just had to get out. I was trying to forget about this while I was still in the tournament and I wasn't being allowed to. I was quite upset in the dressing room but then I was OK.

Again I was two down with three to play and in one of these frames Tony only needed pink and black, but I always get the feeling with Tony, if it gets really close, that he might buckle. He's a very good player, very fluent with a lot of natural ability, but I just don't think he really likes a tough fight.

Beating him took more or less everything I had on top of everything else I had been through. I didn't want to get up the next morning. I was just numb, completely exhausted. I drove to the theatre because I had to, not because I wanted to play. It was 2–2 but Steve made it 6–2 at the end of the first session so it was all over right there. If I could have got through the day just losing by a few frames it wouldn't have been so bad, but by the time it came to the second day he was 12–5 in front and that was just too much.

He made it 17–5 which was 12 up with 13 to play. What was amazing, though, was that suddenly Steve couldn't pot a ball and I won the next frame on the black. The people clapped like crazy. It was the nicest thing about the final. Then Steve won the next to win 18–6. When the last ball went down, he spread his arms out and jumped in the air, which I felt was overdoing it in view of the margin. I felt at the time that he was maybe trying to outdo me by making a bigger gesture than I had made when I dropped on my knees after the 147.

I thought I was supposed to get £18,000 for the 147, but I got £13,000. It was going to be £10,000 for the 147, £5,000 for a new championship record and £3,000 for the highest break. But the way that they looked at it was that I didn't break the championship record because I got a 147! As the championship record was 145, I guess the only way I could have got the £5,000 was to make a 146. Del, who by this time had become the WPBSA's contracts negotiator, as well as managing Higgins and working for BCE, gave me a quick explanation, but I wasn't convinced. I still didn't think it was fair. If they had given me the £5,000, it would have been £18,000 in all for the 147 plus £15,000 for reaching the final. Steve got £30,000 for winning it and I thought it would be great that I was going to win more money than him!

Snooker Scene reported Cliff's progress through the championship

SECOND ROUND

Cliff Thorburn 13, Terry Griffiths 12

Scores – Session 1: 45–72(39); 46–35; 73(34)–42; 151(147)–0; 70(31)–56(44); 51–77(33); 46–90(59); (Thorburn 4–3). Session 2: 73–29; 75(60)–29; 66–27; 37–72; 18–64(54); 67(36)–44; 42–67; (Thorburn 8–6). Session 3: 58–49; 29–77(31); 23–75(33); 79(38)–59; 53(34)–68(68); 106(62)–0; 76(47)–52(32); 54–64; 54(30)–61; 17–113(97); 100(75)–20.

The first and third sessions of this epic contest both produced material for the record books, albeit of a contrasting nature. In the fourth frame of the opening session, Thorburn fluked the initial red and proceeded in 15 minutes, 20 seconds to compile the first 147 break in world championship history. With the possible exception of a couple of angled pots to middle pockets – which are always missable – Thorburn never looked in difficulty although the yellow from its spot with the cue ball between blue spot and middle pocket could not have looked all that easy on 120.

However, Fred Davis's remark, when an enthusiast once tactlessly compared his personal highest of 143 with his elder brother Joe's 147: "It still only won him one frame" was easy to recall when Griffiths, from 1–4, recovered to 3–4 overnight. Thorburn pressed on to 7–3 but at 8–6 – the second session, too, failing to encompass its scheduled number of frames – he was still in a far from commanding position.

Facing a possible 11 frames, the players were unfortunate in that the start of their final session was delayed until 8.55 p.m. by the late finish to the match between Eddie Charlton and John Spencer. "Both of us play it tough," said Griffiths afterwards. "Neither of us rushes round the table. I expected us to take half an hour a frame." The frame which Thorburn won to lead 10–8 occupied, in fact, 65 minutes but when the Canadian, from 10–9, added the next two frames to go three up with four to play the end looked nigh. At 2.18 a.m., in consecutive visits, Thorburn twice unsuccessfully attempted the black which would have would have given him victory at 13–9.

When Griffiths recovered to 10–12, BBC ceased recording, agreed overtime having expired at 2.00 a.m. and, visual record of the match's amazing climax was thus lost to posterity. At 2.56, Thorburn again attempted the black which would have made him a 13–10 winner and after another much more difficult chance had eluded him, a Welsh win suddenly looked possible as Griffiths reached 11–12. At 3.26, Griffiths completed a 97 clearance to level at 12–12 and no praise can therefore be too high for the courage and self-belief that Thorburn displayed when, at his second visit to the table in the decider, he made a break of 75 to assure himself of a place in the quarter-finals.

Some 200 souls remained in the Crucible until the bitter end but with the television cameras idle the atmosphere conveyed the eerie intimacy of a match behind closed doors. Spectators stood up to stretch their legs between frames and even the players and the referee, John Williams, entered into some banter. This was unforgettable for the few who were there but since the championship is now a major national occasion it will be sad, years hence, to have no visual archive material to refer to. At 3.51 a handshake was exchanged. The final session had lasted 6 hours 25 minutes, a record.

QUARTER-FINAL
Cliff Thorburn 13, Kirk Stevens 12

Scores – Session 1: 65–46; 64(39)–34; 80(49)–55(32); 80(66)–9; 21–71(36); 87(40)–33; 5–69(69); 32–66; (Thorburn 5–3). Session 2: 33(32)–90(89); 57–59(30); 105(45)–33; 64–51(34); 12–82(56); 20–99(41, 49); 86(58)–15; (Thorburn 8–7). Session 3: 28–82(65); 56–58(31); 74–66(66); 58(42)–69; 83(83)–8; 2–68(32); 58–64(32); 67(36)–25; 73–29; 85(45)–44.

When Thorburn led 4–0 it seemed highly unlikely that the match would run its full distance but Stevens, having pulled up to 3–5 at the first interval, trailed only 7–8 going into the final session and brought himself to the brink of a famous victory in a marathon final session before Thorburn prevailed.

101

At 1.40 a.m., the match ran into second place in the league table of latest-ever finishes, superseding the epic semi-final of 1979 in which Terry Griffiths beat Eddie Charlton and the final handshake was not offered until 2.12 a.m. after a final session of 6 hours 11 minutes. Despite its inordinate length, the final session offered dramatic content, high quality tactical play and an interplay of contrasting personalities which engrossed the attention throughout.

Stevens was a mere 12 years old when he painstakingly accrued $4 with which to challenge Thorburn, a superstar even then, 13 years ago, in the unreported sub-culture from which Canadian snooker had not even begun to emerge. Thorburn disclaimed the $4 when he won but Stevens thrust it upon him. Thus was instigated an elder brother/younger brother relationship founded on mutual respect, which has endured through clashes of personality and which has survived the rivalrous feelings which naturally loomed large when the younger man narrowed the ability gap.

Stevens won the first two frames of the final session, the latter with a spectacularly fluked black, to lead 9–8 but his first break of 66 in the next frame amazingly proved insufficient to avert a black ball defeat. Refusing to be cast down, Stevens went to 10–9 by winning the kind of grinding 50 minute frame which is a Thorburn speciality, but again the former world champion responded with a frame-winning break of 83 to reach 10–10.

A frame ahead for the third time, Stevens at last managed to widen the gap to two with a clearance which gave him victory on the black and a 12–10 lead, but even from two up with three to play he proved unable to clinch his second appearance in a world semi-final. Exemplifying grit, application and an obstinate aversion to losing, Thorburn patiently accrued two frames of 32 and 53 minutes respectively to level at 12–12.

The 60 minute deciding frame which gave him his 13–12 victory over Eddie Charlton on his way to his – as it proved – unsuccessful appearance in the 1977 final against John Spencer sprang to mind as the decider developed on cautious tactical lines. Stevens led by a dozen points but, consummate match player that he is, Thorburn produced a priceless break of 45, negotiating many tricky positions until, sinking the last red with the aid of the half-butt spider, he needed to pot only a simple black to leave his opponent pursuing two snookers. One four point penalty was duly obtained and there was a fleeting possibility of another, but after 61 minutes play another duration record for a deciding frame, Thorburn was able to walk out of the arena and into the semi-finals.

SEMI-FINAL
Cliff Thorburn 16 Tony Knowles 15

Scores – Session 1: 74(74)–51(33); 58–30; 13–89(51); 15–94(52, 34); 56–50; 42(38)–98; 52–56(37); 14–66(36); (Knowles 5–3). Session 2: 60–53(31); 64(31)–27; 8–89(48, 34); 9–66(40); 71(32)–32; 59(37)–18; 23–58(34); (Knowles 8–7). Session 3: 85(32)–32; 76–33(32); 49–55(30); 72(35)–8; 39–65(40); 64(30)–48; 66(41)–49(33); (Thorburn 12–10). Session 4: 50–61; 41–50; 35–79(74); 66–21; 47–59(33); 29–57; 70–58(36); 64–31; 68–37.

Those who expected Thorburn to show any adverse reaction from playing half the previous night were disappointed. In the opening frame, Knowles potted every ball he attempted and sent the cue ball to within an inch of the baulk cushion from those he did not. In this way, Knowles proceeded to 51–0 but one safety shot fell short of perfection and Thorburn cleared the table with a break of 74. This proved to be the Canadian's highest break of the match and the high quality of this opening frame was rarely matched by subsequent frames.

From 2–3; Knowles won the last three frames of the opening session to lead 5–3 overnight, but the Canadian, aided by a tie-break black in the first frame of the day, levelled at 5–5 and again 7–7 after Knowles had once more gone two frames ahead.

Poised for a clearance which, with the last red, black and all the colours, would have enabled him to tie, Thorburn snookered himself on the red in the last frame of the second session. He escaped without penalty and left the red in a position from which his opponent was not certain to pot it, but so angry was he at having lost position that he conceded the frame forthwith.

Thorburn won the first two frames of the penultimate session but failed at a relatively easy pink which would have give him 10–8. However, at 11–10 it was Knowles's turn to make a crucial error as he miscued on the last red to allow the 1980 champion to clear to the pink and lead 12–10 going into the final session.

Knowles won the first two frames of the final session in pink ball finishes and with a break of 74 went one up. Uncertain in his potting, lacking fluency in his break-building, Thorburn kept in contention only through the quality of his safety play and the force of his personality. He levelled at 13–13 but Knowles again went one up by taking the last red, blue and all the colours to win on the black.

Knowles looked on the very brink of the final when Thorburn, needing the colours to win the next frame, snookered himself on the blue, but even from two up with three to play Knowles could not make it an all-English final. Within two pots of clinching the match in the following frame, Knowles faltered on the pink as his lead was cut to 15–14. Two more clearcut match-winning chances came his way in the following frame but he lost position on 22 early on with the balls wide open and later miscued on the last red as the contest reached 15–15.

The deciding frame was, at 43 minutes, appreciably shorter than the 61 minutes decider Thorburn had played against Stevens but it followed the same pattern, each ball a struggle, each shot selection a mental board meeting. Understandably shaky, Knowles failed at the penultimate red when it lay in the jaws of a pocket and eventually the gods smiled on the dogged, as Thorburn, fluking the last red, proceeded to what proved the winning position of 20 in front of the blue. The final session was one of 4 hours, 45 minutes play.

FINAL
Steve Davis 18 Cliff Thorburn 6

Scores – Session 1: 82–20; 11–112(34, 49); 83–39; 36–80; 80(48)–34; 65–34; 81(60)–44; 75(33)–26; (Davis 6–2). Session 2: 82(33, 30)–6; 73(59)–0; 81–48(47); 41–67(33); 25–71(55); 100(92)–8; 15–68(54); 96(41, 49)–2; 76–47; (Davis 12–5). Session 3: 58–53; 75–28; 62(59)–47; 67(43)–62(37); 131(131)–0; 24–62; 77(56)–70(37).

The first four frames were evenly split but, from 32–34, Davis took the fifth with a 48 clearance and never looked back, winning the remaining frames of the opening session and the first three on the resumption to lead 9–2. At 12–5 overnight, with Davis dauntingly solid, only one result looked possible.

The pink would have given Thorburn the first frame of the final day and he was also on the verge of winning both the third and fourth, in the latter of which he needed to pot only a simple penultimate red to leave Davis needing a snooker. However, he had been denied by Davis's 59 clearance to the pink in the previous frame and in this he was overtaken by the 43 clearance which gave Davis victory on the black.

Davis went 12 up with 13 to play with a classic total clearance of 131 but even then Thorburn fought on, a tactical frame of 39 minutes giving him his only success of the day before Davis took the next on a tie-break black to clinch the title. So pronounced was Davis's command that few regretted the early finish.

WHERE THE MONEY WENT

Champion:	Steve Davis	£30,000
Runner-up:	Cliff Thorburn	£15,000
Losing semi-finalists:	Alex Higgins, Tony Knowles	£8,400
Losing quarter-finalists:	Bill Werbenuik, Eddie Charlton	
	Kirk Stevens, Tony Meo	£4,450
Second round losers:	Willie Thorne, David Taylor,	
	John Spencer, Dennis Taylor,	
	Terry Griffiths, Perrie Mans,	
	Doug Mountjoy, Ray Reardon	£2,950
First round losers:	Dean Reynolds, John Virgo,	
	Dave Martin, Jiro Meadowcroft,	

	Les Dodd, Mike Hallett, Silvino Francisco, Rex Williams, John Campbell, Mark Wildman, Ian Black, Mick Fisher, Cliff Wilson, Jimmy White, Graham Miles, Eugene Hughes	£1,500
Highest break:	Cliff Thorburn – 147	£3,000
		plus
	Special award	£10,000

The day after the final I was in no shape to fly home, but the following day I drove Darryl McKerrow to Manchester airport before I drove back to London. At least that was the idea but the engine on my car blew up. I stopped off at a gas station and

I am not feeling as fresh as I look in this picture taken just before the start of the 1983 world final against Steve Davis

said to this guy: "Here, sell this car for me. Just get what you can for it." It was a 1976–7 Jag. I trusted him. The fellow sold it and he sent me the money. He also drove me from Coventry to Robert Winsor's house in North London. I gave him the chalk I made the 147 with.

I had met Robert playing golf two or three years earlier. He was my partner that day. We were playing with Jimmy Tarbuck and somebody at Wentworth. I made a 15-foot putt on the last green to save him £20 and we've been friends ever since. We started to play golf and go out to dinner together and I always enjoyed his company. He knows how to enjoy himself, but he's always there at the desk at 9 o'clock the next morning. He became my manager in 1985 but at this time we had no business relationship. Robert certainly didn't need to manage a snooker player because he's made millions from his own business, point of sale advertising. He came with me to some of my matches and he was at Wembley when I won the Benson and Hedges that year.

That summer I hardly played at all, but I was really fit and relaxed and won the Winfield Masters in Australia with virtually no practice. Some of the arrangements were like the bad old days in England when everything had to stop for television. We actually played the event in the studios of Channel 10 and everything was rehearsed. There was even a floor manager standing in for me rehearsing the answers in the after-match interview: "Were you happy with the way you played, Cliff?" "Well I . . ."

Television called an interval between every frame while they edited the previous frame and recorded the links. We just stood about losing concentration so after the third frame I walked off to the dressing room and told them to come and get me when they were ready. Another thing they didn't get quite right was that the players' chairs were high cocktail stools.

I beat Warren King, Jimmy White and Kirk Stevens to get to the final and then I beat Bill Werbeniuk 7–3 to win it. It was a very happy tournament. We played golf one day and Tony Knowles spent so much time in the bunkers that I christened him Tony of Arabia. We went to a reception one day where there was this enormous ham got up to look like a snooker table. Dennis (Taylor) had only just stopped by because he was going on somewhere to play an exhibition. We both got our cues out to pose for a picture pointing our tips at the cue ball on the ham and Dennis just lost his concentration for a second. Suddenly, he realised that his tip had gone right inside the glazing so off he went to play his exhibition with glazing stuck to his tip. I never did ask him how he made out.

The referee was Ron Tcherne, who had his own method of marking a ball which had to be cleaned. He would just remove one of the colours from its spot and use this to mark the position of the ball he was cleaning. On the last day Ron departed early from our champagne breakfast. "We'll send you a ball marker for Christmas," Tony Knowles shouted after him.

I made a 128 against Kirk in the semi-final which took the $2,000 high break prize, but I had to share it with Bill. There was $10,000 for a 147 and in the fifth frame, when I was leading 3–1, Bill got up to 13 reds, 13 blacks. For about three minutes he stared at his next red. It was easy to stay on the black or the blue. Finally, he starts laughing, turns to me and says: "What do you wanna do? Do you wanna save on this? If I make a 147 we'll make $5,000 each, but if I miss I get half the high break you've got now."

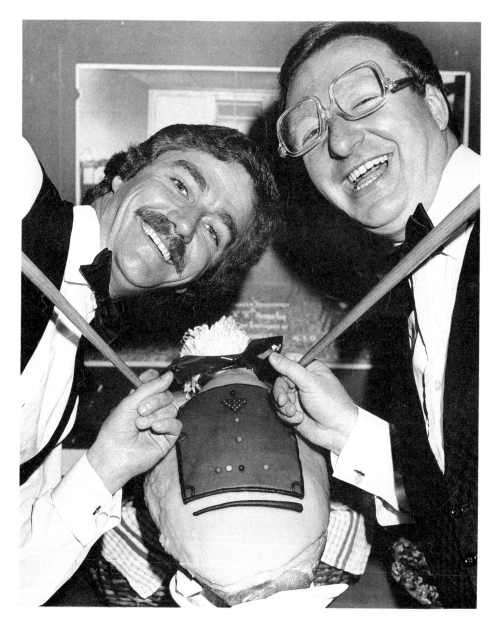

With Dennis Taylor at the Winfield Masters in Sydney. Just after this picture was taken Dennis poked his cue-tip into the glazed part of this ham by mistake. He didn't smile so much then

This negotiation was taking place on television. I sat there in the chair thinking how I would feel if he missed right then, or after one more red or something, but I said: "OK, go for the 147." He knocked in the red with the rest and missed a half ball black. He thought this was very funny. I was steaming.

In this tournament I went for a lot of balls that I normally wouldn't go for and most of them went in. I played like that in my first match of the 1983–4 British season, the Langs Scottish Masters, when I beat Terry Griffiths 5–1 and also when I lost 6–2 to Tony Knowles in the semi-finals. I didn't use this game plan again. If it had worked, I'd still be doing it.

The 1983–4 season wasn't all that bad in terms of results, but it wasn't very satisfying. After 1982–3, when I won the Masters, made the 147 at Sheffield and got to the final of the world championship, I guess I didn't work quite so hard or with the same sense of incentive as I would have done if 1982–3 had been a bad season. It's hard to be sharp in your mind and your approach if you're not working towards a specific target. You do your best in each match as it comes along, but if there's no specific aim or ambition you just tend to drift.

There was the basic problem of commuting from Canada unless I was prepared not to see Barb and Jamie for months on end. The only alternative was to move to England again and we didn't feel ready for that. And unless you're really clear and strong in your mind, little things upset you which normally you would shrug off. There were also things that were not so little because as soon as you have a wife and children it bothers you if anything is the matter with them. To play my best snooker I need all the basics of life to be OK so that I can feel that snooker is more important than anything else. Of course, it isn't, but I need to feel that way to channel my concentration.

In the Jameson International at Newcastle, I was two down to Dennis Taylor and then 3–1 down and beat him 5–3. It took about five hours but it did bug me that the press started to talk about a time limit per shot idea. To put all the blame on me was really absurd and I couldn't help thinking that when I had tried to play a little quicker nobody had made any comment about it.

I know I'm tagged as a slow player and I've had a couple of accusations, even from one of my closest friends on the circuit, that I was deliberately trying to slow the game down. Maybe when I played for money it was different, but there's no way that I could do that in a professional game. It would affect me more than the other guy. With the people that I used to gamble with, I used to say "to hell with it" I'll play at my own pace, not to bore the guy to death but to blank him out in a way because he had nothing to do with my personal business there. The money in my pocket was mine.

Anyway, in the next round of the Jameson, I beat Doug Mountjoy 5–2 and in the semi-final Terry Griffiths 9–8 after being three down with four to play. Steve beat me in the final 9–4. I missed the black to lose the last frame of the afternoon which would have put me 5–3 down at the interval instead of 6–2. There was another frame when I jumped the cue ball over the black with the balls wide open. Afterwards, Dickie Davies of ITV said: "Well, Cliff, you must feel bad about that performance".

I said without thinking: "Yes, I could have got beat by five or six players". This sounded much worse than I really meant it to, but at the back of my mind I still did feel that, even playing like that, not all that many players would have beaten me.

It was a big surprise on paper when I then lost 5–1 to Joe Johnson in the Professional Players Tournament at Bristol. Joe was nobody special then, but he played absolutely great against me, just like he did in the world championship in 1986. He also beat Jimmy White, Eddie Charlton and Tony Meo and lost 9–8 in the final to Tony Knowles. In the semi-finals, the bookies had him 10–1 so I stuck £100 on him to win.

Bill, Kirk and I then lost to England in the semi-finals of the world cup and a couple of weeks later I lost 5–1 to Silvino Francisco in the qualifying competition of the Lada Classic, which became a ranking tournament that year.

Barb miscarried that day for the second time that year. We were staying with friends in London. I drove up to Warrington in the morning and I went straight back that night. Barb was in bad shape, haemorrhaging badly, much worse than when she lost the baby during the world championship. After two miscarriages, you do think it might be the end of the road and this was Barb's second in six months but they found out that her ovary was dilating too soon. With our second child she was stitched up and they had to hope that the stitch held.

We went home and I came back for the world doubles at Northampton. John Virgo and I got to the semi-finals. We were 7–7 with Tony Knowles and Jimmy White when Tony made a foul. John was due to play next, but didn't like the position so he asked Tony to play again. That was fine but in some way the 'play again' confused us. When Tony had played, I came to the table. I concentrated hard on quite a difficult red, shook out the black and several more reds from the bunch and then heard the referee call foul. I had played out of order and Jimmy made 74 from the position I would have had to go 8–7. I was clearing up in the next frame when I had a kick so we lost 9–7.

By this time, I was one of Air Canada's best customers. I went home for Christmas and came back for the Benson and Hedges Masters in late-January. I felt sharp and I led John Spencer 4–1. I guess I got complacent and he beat me 5–4. It was fixed for John and I to go back to Robert's house for dinner and maybe this was part of the reason my concentration just went. John enjoyed dinner more than I did.

This was the tournament that Kirk made his 147 in the semi-finals. One of the amazing things about it was that Donald Sutherland, the great Canadian actor, wanted to see what tournament snooker was like and showed up just in time for the frame when Kirk made the maximum. He had to go on somewhere else so the 147 was the only frame he got to see. He probably thinks snooker's like that all the time.

I beat Meo and lost to Knowles in the Tolly Cobbold Classic in Ipswich and went home again to find that my father and stepmother were both ill. My stepmother had broken her arm and leg in a fall. My father ended up with a bleeding ulcer. They live in Windsor, Ontario, and I had to go up to look after my father for four or five days while he was in hospital. I tried to cancel out of the Benson and Hedges Irish Masters, but Del said that I wasn't allowed to. I flew to Dublin the day before and I flew home the day after I lost 5–2 to Dennis Taylor. This cost me at least £2,000. A couple of years later Kirk didn't show up because he missed his flight from Heathrow and was fined £500. I guess it would have been cheaper if I had done this. All the trips backwards and forwards across the Atlantic were making me fed up, although of course it wouldn't have been so bad if I'd been winning.

In the championship I beat Mario Morra 10–3 and Willie Thorne 13–11, playing OK but nothing special. I lost 13–8 to Jimmy White in the quarters and my season was over. During the summer, I went to Australia and New Zealand again which was enjoyable but, from a playing point of view, a non-event. I lost to Willie Thorne in the untelevised phase of the Winfield Masters and spent the next couple of weeks with Dennis Taylor, who had also lost in the first round. We practised a bit but mostly we had a good time and ate like kings. We had both put on about 12 pounds when we got to New Zealand.

The schedule was for two matches in each session and Jimmy White was on before I had to play David Taylor in the second match. I was just getting out of the bath when the phone rang and I was told I was playing in 15 minutes. I got dressed except for doing up my waistcoat. One minute before the match, I got to do it up and I can't get the buttons fastened. When I bent over, I just couldn't breath. I felt dizzy. I got beat 3–0 and I was just glad to get out of there.

I went to Government House in Ottawa that summer to be presented with the Order of Canada by the Governor General, Ed Schreyer. It was very nice to be recognised in this way. Being a snooker player had been such a stigma to carry in my early days that this kinda made up for it. It also turned out that Ed Schreyer was a snooker nut with his own table.

Barb and I at Government House, Ottawa with the Governor-General, Ed Schreyer, who presented me with the Order of Canada

EIGHT

GETTING BACK

THAT SUMMER of 1983, I lost 9–6 to Frank Jonik in the semi- final of the Canadian championship. Frank also beat Jim Wych and he had his chance to beat Kirk in the final which Kirk eventually won 9–8. I also re-assessed my game after what had been a poor season. I had slipped back and I could see that unless I did something about it I would slip back even further. I was just fed up with the way I was playing and went back to my old style, choking up – shortening my grip – when I was in round the pink and black and lengthening the grip for the long shots. I managed to get myself a bit more clear-headed and I came back to Britain for 1984–5 with a much better attitude. It's great to feel yourself moving forward again and to feel that after playing for 20 years I could still improve. I woke up in the mornings looking forward to playing snooker.

Steve beat me 5–2 in my first match in the Langs and I lost 5–0 to John Virgo in the Jameson International, when I was streaming with cold and John played well. There was some edge to the match on John's side because I had entered the world doubles with Willie Thorne instead of him. But this was only because I had heard that Geoff Lomas, who was running a string of players then, was wanting to team up John with Tony Knowles.

From the Jameson at Newcastle I went to the pre-televised phase of the Rothmans at Bristol and almost lost to Gino Rigitano, who is one of a dozen or so Canadians who are about half-way up the rankings. At 4–2 I was coasting but then I lost two frames and was 42–0 down in the decider. I made 42, missed a green which could have cost me the match and struggled home on the colours. Until it was 0–42, it hadn't sunk in that I could lose.

I beat Tony Meo 5–4, Doug Mountjoy 5–3 and then Steve 9–7 which gave me great satisfaction. Steve had just won the Langs and the Jameson but he said after

I'd beaten him that he knew it was going to be close because he didn't feel as if he was playing very well! He led 6–3. I made it 6–6. He led 7–6 and then I won three in a row. Steve did say afterwards: "It's the best I've seen Cliff play for ages and he didn't let me play well".

Although it was a long match, I didn't feel shattered from playing Steve when I played Dennis in the final the next day. It was just unfortunate for me that Dennis was absolutely inspired. He was knocking in the long shots and screwing back like he never had before and he just broke me. It was 2–2 and he slaughtered me 10–2. He played as if he just knew it was his time to win a big title. Dennis was virtually unbeatable that day but I felt ready to win something. Maybe if the next tournament had been anywhere but Preston I would have, but something always seems to go wrong there and 1984 was just awful.

Just after I'd beaten Cliff Wilson in the second round, I heard that Darryl McKerrow had died. He was not just my manager but a good friend and obviously the first thing I thought of was whether I should quit the tournament and go back home. Barb talked with Darryl's wife and we all thought it was best just to keep on playing. Once I had decided to play, I would have loved to have won the tournament.

What made it even worse was that I just couldn't believe that Darryl had died in such a bizarre way. He was up in Manitoba about 1500 miles from Toronto for a few days' hunting. The group of guys that he was with were all in this hut and a few of them would go out and hunt. They'd been warned that they shouldn't go out at night. Darryl went out, killed a deer and skinned it on the spot. So he had to carry a 60 to 80 pound deer back about half a mile to the hut. He sat down for a rest, fell asleep and of course it was snowing so much he was covered in snow in a couple of hours. The others went looking for him and found him. He was still alive next day and he was mumbling: "Darryl, Darryl, what have you done?" Then he died of a heart attack that day.

When I played Ray Reardon, I was numb. He was ahead 8–4 but then, just when I had nothing to lose at all, my game sort of clicked and Ray got anxious. I won five in a row to win 9–8.

This put me into the semi-finals against Higgins. I was ahead 6–5 and I lost 9–7 and once again Higgins got under my skin. In the 12th frame, I snookered myself. I nominated green but John Smyth, who was the referee, didn't hear me and called a foul. Naturally, I said that I had nominated so the referee then asked Higgins. He said that he watched my mouth all the time when I played and that I definitely hadn't said anything. So then I asked the referee to ask the crowd and about ten people said that I had nominated, but Higgins still said that he hadn't heard.

I felt the referee was very intimidated by Higgins and I was steaming because Alex wouldn't take my word for it as I would have took his. Snooker players do have a code and I have played by it all my life. I've played long enough to know you give the benefit of doubt to your opponent in situations like that. I called out Paul Hatherell, who was the tournament director, and explained everything. He then went over to John Smyth and Smyth said that he didn't think that I had nominated. Paul just said that the referee's decision was final and walked away. It was very easy for him. So there we were with ten people who had heard me, the referee who hadn't and Alex, who said he was watching my mouth.

The shot itself was insignificant. The seven-point penalty made virtually no difference because I hadn't left a free ball but the whole incident completely threw me. I was angry and I also felt saddened for Alex and his stupid attitude. This coming on top of Darryl dying and trying to weigh the significance of both these things just left me with no heart for the battle. If I had been perfect I would have put it completely out of my mind but who's perfect?

After the match, I was determined not to say anything in the press conference that I might regret. In fact, I'm always very careful what I say in press conferences because some journalists are always just waiting for a chance to write something that will stir up bad feeling. So all I said was: "I should have said it louder. My mistake. It was my fault that I kept thinking about it. I've played to a code all my life. It seems that Alex doesn't." Still this wasn't enough for some of them. Straight after I had said this, some guy I'd never seen before said: "Do you think that Higgins is a cheat?"

Willie Thorne and I got to the final of the Hofmeister World Doubles beating John Virgo and Kirk Stevens in the quarters and Tony Knowles and John Spencer 9–1 in the semis. We lost 10–2 in the final to Higgins and Jimmy White. During this and over Christmas I stayed with Willie and Fiona Thorne in Leicester. We practised together, had a few laughs and, from my point of view, probably got a bit too pally. I was just on the point of signing a contract for Robert to manage me and he was saying that I play my best when I don't actually hate my opponent but when I can feel a real hard competitive edge. I certainly found it hard to feel this kind of edge with Willie, though of course I wanted to beat him when we both got to the final of the Mercantile Credit Classic in January 1985.

It was a great tournament for Willie because he beat Steve Davis 9–8 in the semi-finals. I had come through a lot of tough matches beating Steve Longworth 5–3 from 3–3 and Terry Griffiths 5–4 from 4–2 down. Terry and I got through just after midnight. I think it was the earliest we have ever finished. One reason we have long matches is that we each know what the other is going to do shot for shot. I don't think much about his problems or his game, but it does strike me that he's almost too nice a guy to be playing this game. Drinking tea the way he does while you're playing in the world championship just doesn't add up. He was always telling me how fed up he was going around playing all the time. He does treat snooker as if it's a job, as if it really is work. I'm not sure if he really enjoys what he's doing. Maybe winning the championship at his first try is something to do with him not having more success. He could only go down after that. It's almost like the game is bigger than he really wants it to be. I think he'd still rather play just at weekends. He's also got the longest cue action in the game and a very long bridge for lots of shots. I think that the reason that John Spencer has gone right down, even before his eye problems, is because of his long cue action. There was too much that could go wrong.

After I'd beaten Terry in the quarters I beat Joe Johnson 9–2 in the semis so there were Willie and I in the final. Willie led 8–7 after two sessions. I had played very well in the first session to lead 4–3 and I was a little surprised after two not just that Willie was still with me but that he was a frame ahead. For the final session on the Sunday afternoon my concentration was very bad. I don't know why exactly but it may have been something to do with the fact that Willie's parents were sat up on the stage very prominently and all his pals were there as well. I've been in this situation many times and often it's made little or no difference, but this time I just couldn't get totally into myself as I needed to kill him if I got the chance. I won the first frame on the last afternoon, but overall in that session I played very badly. I think I played to stun in three balls along the black ball cushion instead of floating the cue ball through and going off two cushions. I missed them all and they cost me frames. Willie kept himself together quite well and that was it, 13–8.

Three finals and a semi-final in my last four tournaments still wasn't bad, though, and then I won the Masters at Wembley for the second time. I made a break of 103 in the first frame of the tournament, which I'm told is unique, and it turned out to be the only century of the week. I beat Ray Reardon 5–0 in the quarters and Jimmy White 6–4 in the semi after being three down.

Jimmy is a great favourite of the Wembley crowd and in particular of a section of it which always seems to back either him or Higgins. A few of these characters sometimes go too far. They had upset Willie when he was playing Jimmy in the first round by calling out: "Why don't you go home, Willie". I was a bit apprehensive about how I would be treated but actually the crowd were very good with me that night. It was a very good match and, as always, it was very stimulating to play Jimmy. You can be in control of the play for 90 per cent of the time and lose on just one shot. If you lose your concentration with him, you're gone because there's no time to recover. I get more sense of achievement out of beating him than I do with most players because he's so difficult to keep at bay. On top of that, he's such a pleasure to play because he's such a gentleman, such a good sport. There's never any aggro. Win or lose, nothing fazes him.

Doug Mountjoy came through the other side of the draw, which not many people expected, but he's never easy to beat because he plays like me. He never gives up. I led 6–3 but he got back to 6–5. I won 9–6. Even though the match hadn't gone the distance, it was after midnight when we finished.

At the Dulux British Open at Derby, I lost 5–2 to Higgins in the last 16. At 2–2, he shook my hand, which I thought was peculiar. I said: "Are we playing best of five or what?" Next frame he made a 142. The last frame was 65 minutes, included 21 minutes on the yellow, which only goes to show that Alex can grind out the safety when he has to. In fact, as he's got older, his potting has deteriorated, but he's made up for this in other ways.

Silvino Francisco beat Higgins in the one semi and Kirk beat Steve Davis 9–7 in the other. Silvino was ahead of Kirk 8–3 and 9–5 at the end of the first day. On the last afternoon the whole thing turned sour. Kirk caught up to 9–8 but Silvino was convinced that Kirk was high on drugs. Silvino himself was in a very emotional state because it was his first major final. He had been winning easily and now it looked as if he could lose. Between frames, Silvino followed Kirk to the toilet and gave him a piece of his mind. This was very bad. What was absolutely inexcusable was that he pushed Kirk about and shook him to make his listen to what he was saying. This is a taboo: you must never actually touch your opponent. No one knows if this changed the course of the match any more than Silvino could have known for sure whether Kirk was high or not. Anyway, Silvino won 12–9.

The WPBSA mishandled the whole thing. If there had been an immediate inquiry, I believe Silvino should have been fined for what he did to Kirk. But nothing happened until the whole thing came out in the newspapers. Then Silvino was fined £6,000 – which I thought was a little strong – and then it turned out that

114

the WPBSA had not gone through all the proper processes. Everything dragged on until there was a re-trial in front of a QC. What all this cost I have no idea but the WPBSA lost a lot of credibility along the way.

It was obvious that the WPBSA were not controlling the game as they should have done. The trouble is that the board are either players or the people who represent them. The board members usually vote, when it comes down to it, for what is best for them or out of some personal friendship. It all gets very personal and the game suffers. A few years ago, I was on the board. The system at this time was that the world's top ten automatically were the board. This was obviously farcical. I remember sitting there one day listening to Reardon and Spencer droning on for hours and thinking: "What am I doing here when I could be on the golf course?"

Other sports seem to get retired players or semi-retired players or people successful in other walks of life to run things and it would be better if snooker could somehow get into this situation. Just as players, everybody gets along pretty well. The trouble comes when players try to be officials or promoters or politicians as well. As it is, there seems to be a lot of scheming and what is considered fair by someone on the board isn't always considered fair by someone who isn't on the board. I don't think anyone has done anything deliberately against me but at least twice, when I was No 2, the seeding system was altered to my disadvantage. But, then again, my manager isn't on the board.

The business with Silvino and Kirk really got the press into the snooker and drugs angle. Drug testing was introduced – the main idea being to make sure that players didn't take drugs which were against the law – and then it came out that some players were taking beta blockers, which aren't against the law but which are banned in archery and shooting because they are supposed to slow the heart beat, steady the nerves and reduce anxiety. Bill Werbeniuk was taking them at one time because all the lager he was drinking was speeding up his heart beat and he needed beta blockers to slow it down a bit.

I think that what players do in private is their own business, but I don't think that anybody should be allowed to take drugs to help them play better.

I lost to Jimmy White in the Benson and Hedges Irish Masters and went home to prepare for the championship. Up in Grimsby, Mike Hallett was preparing for it as well and when we met at Sheffield he was obviously readier than I was. He was ahead 6–1 and if I hadn't managed to win the last two frames of that session there wouldn't have been much point showing up the next day. When you're down something like 6–1, you've just got to win the first frame on the comeback trail and then hope to win three of the next four. If you can do that it's 7–5 and anybody's match.

At 7–4, Mike led 52–1. I fluked a red – I fluke about three balls a session – and made 33 from it. Eventually Mike had a chance at a long brown for 8–4 but I cleared up to get back to 7–5. I think Mike lost his head a bit at this stage. He's matured a bit now but then, if things weren't going well for him the balls could be scattered from here to Vancouver. He also played much too fast for his own good sometimes. He's always been a very good potter and genuinely believes now that he can beat a top player whereas when he played me that time it seemed like he only thought he *might* beat me.

I kept battling. Mike gradually lost his belief and I won 10–8. A year later, Mike showed that he had learnt something from this experience when he beat Dennis Taylor, then the defending champion, 10–8 in the first round. His safety play was a little better, his attitude was more positive and he didn't panic quite so much when he started losing a big lead.

I went through to the quarter-finals by beating Bill Werbeniuk 13–3. Bill had lost the form which had made him so formidable a couple of seasons earlier and I couldn't help thinking that he was going to have to stop drinking the quantity of lager that he was taking to combat the shake in his cue arm which he said was some hereditary problem. Some time in the late Sixties, Bill was in a car accident which severed his little finger and when he came back from this he was having trouble holding his cue steady because there was a raw nerve ending. Whether his problem was hereditary or whether it was caused by this car crash really makes no difference. Either way, Bill felt that he had got to start drinking hours before the match to get himself into a state where he could control the shake in his cue arm. I used to be sorry for him when we'd be there having bacon and eggs for breakfast while Bill had already been up two hours before that drinking beer to get himself ready for the match.

Dennis Taylor then beat me 13–5. The press were quick to tell me that the first session had been 4 hours 14 minutes for six frames and the second 5 hours 31 minutes for nine frames. Bu this time Dennis was 10–5 up. He wasn't playing as well as he did to beat Steve in that great final but he was playing pretty tight and not making many mistakes.

The key game was when he was ahead 8–5. Jim Thorpe was refereeing and called a push shot on me. I didn't think it was, but Dennis cleared up from there to make it 9–5 and won the last frame of the night as well. If I could have won those two frames to make it 8–7 it could have been different but 10–5 down was just too much. I didn't win a frame next day. When the press started thinking about how long the match had taken, I said: "I wasn't the only one who played safe. If I'd played well this would have been the longest match ever."

In the last four or five years, the snooker circuit has got tighter and tighter with tournaments. I guess it won't be long before a player can play tournaments 50 weeks a year if he wants to – or if he can take it. I can still take it pretty easy in the summers – a whole lot easier than I can take the winters – but once the season gets going everything revolves round your next match. If you win most of them, you practise, prepare, rest, play, eat, sleep and not much else, at least not much else that sticks in your mind. I once read a magazine article – a Day in the Life of Dennis Taylor or something like that. It made me think that if Dennis had many days like that he soon wouldn't be able to play at all. In fact, about half-way through the year he was champion, he just faded out because he was mentally exhausted.

Concentration is very important and you need time to settle into it. If you've got 20 things buzzing round your mind you can't just shut them off an hour before your match. On a match day, if I'm playing at two o'clock or three o'clock, I'll wake up about 8.30 and watch some news on TV. I'll get up and shower and often I'll take breakfast in my room. Breakfast downstairs might be okay if I knew who I was having it with but if not it can mean aggravation of some sort. After breakfast, I'll read my book – just five or six pages – and my mind will be moving towards practising at around 11.30 or the match itself. On match days, I try to do everything a little more slowly than I usually do whether it's eating, brushing my teeth, shaving or anything. I consciously slow everything down because the worst thing I can do to myself is rush.

I'll practise about an hour, just building up my rhythm and co-ordination, concentrating on getting the cue through straight, and then I'll go back to my room and lie down. I'll think some more about the match, picturing the kind of situations I might be in, especially at the start of games, and I'll think about my own game, just going through in my mind what I have to do. This is exciting isn't it?

You might think that after all these years that I would just know how to play and just go there and do it but it's very important to me to tune myself in. I won't want to get too interested in anything else that is happening so until it's time for me to go to the venue I'll just lie on the bed and think. Or just lie on the bed. If I do this, I usually feel fresh and keen for the match.

If I'm playing afternoon and evening sessions the same day, I'll take my tuxedo with me. I won't want to rush back to the hotel between sessions to change when I could be lying on a couch in my dressing room. If I'm playing at 10.30 in the morning, I like to be awake at 6.30. I've found from experience it's best to be awake for abour four hours before I start to play a match. This isn't that easy if it's been 2.00 or 2.30 before I get to bed. All this may seem very boring. I'm not bored by it because it's the way I build up to play. But if I did this without playing the matches I'd go crazy.

Preparing for the 1985–6 season, I beat Jim Wych and Bob Chaperon in the last two rounds of the Canadian championship, both 6–4. They were very good matches. The overall standard was higher than it had ever been before. At the Langs Scottish Masters I beat Silvino Francisco 6–0 in the semi-finals, a session as good as any I ever played in that kind of style. I had total clearance of 133 and 142 and the six frames took only 99 minutes. "You can call me the fastest of the slower players now or else the slowest of the faster players," I quipped at the press conference.

In the afternoon of the final against Willie, who'd beaten Dennis Taylor and Jimmy White, I never missed a ball and led 5–2. Willie played very well in the evening and led 7–6, but I won the last three to close him out 9–7. Willie and I were having quite a few matches round about this time. He's got a lot of ability and when he's flowing he makes it all look very easy, but deep down he's a bit lazier than most of the leading players, not as dedicated. He tends to put defeats down to reasons which aren't really relevant. I used to think that his practice wasn't doing him all that much good because he'd just smash the pack up and try to make century breaks. I play loose in practice but only up to a point. I still break normally because, in professional snooker, how often are all 15 reds spread nicely all round the table? Then, Willie started to learn the safety game and I think he's trying to simulate match conditions in practice much more now. Practice is not match play whatever you do to it but you do have to practise with a method and, if you're playing with an opponent, play frames of a pattern and rhythm which are sometimes like match frames.

I came down to Stoke for the Goya, which replaced the Jameson, and could have lost to Dave Martin. It was 3–3 and I was 0–62 down. Dave can pot balls as well as anybody, but lacks a bit of confidence when it comes to winning a tournament or beating a top player. He and David Taylor are prime examples of players who have played the same way all their lives. They're waiting in their minds for something to happen before they get better. Their game gets them so far, but there's no extra gear.

John Campbell I beat 5–0 and Steve Duggan 5–2 after it had been 2–2. Duggan, in fact, had beaten Willie. It was pretty close for most of the semi-final against Dennis before I won 9–5. There was one frame where I fouled and Dennis couldn't make his mind up about whether to make me play again or not. So he said: "If I make you go again, you won't pot it will you?"

I said: "You'll regret it".

We went back and forth with a couple of comments until finally he made me play again. I smashed a red in and in some strange way this incident seemed to spur me on because I won four frames in a row for the match.

Jimmy White had beaten Steve Davis in the quarter-finals and Neal Foulds in the semis. We played best of 23 and at the first interval he led 7–0. It was the finest exhibition of snooker I've ever seen. I see from looking at the scores that he didn't make a century, but that doesn't mean anything. He just didn't miss. I didn't feel bad. I didn't feel demoralised because I hadn't had the chance to play badly.

During the interval, Paul Hatherell, who was tournament director, asked Robert what we were going to do for the crowd for the final session. I guess he thought it wouldn't take Jimmy too long to win five more frames. In the first frame of the second session, Jimmy led 74–0 with only four reds left. He then jumped the cue ball off the table in potting one of them so in a way this was worse, 70 behind with three reds. As it was the first frame of a new session, I just wanted to play a few shots to get the feel of the table and just possibly slow Jimmy down a bit, but some of the snookers I laid turned out to be good ones. Two of them left me free balls and I ended up with a 42 clearance to win on the black.

By far the hardest part of all that was to run out the colours because it's not always easy to make that mental adjustment from assuming that you've lost to suddenly, out of the blue, realising that you've only got to do something quite straightforward to win.

It was still 7–1 to Jimmy but the game was worth five to me. *Snooker Scene* said: "White's feeling of omnipotence was shaken, and Thorburn's self-esteem refurbished". Actually, I think Jimmy was just very embarrassed and irritated about losing that frame. I noticed the difference in him right away and he only won one frame that session so it was 8–6 to him when we came back for the final session the next afternoon.

Jimmy won the first frame to make it 9–6 but I made a century the next frame and won five in a row. I won 12–10. I remember Jimmy telling the press afterwards: "When Cliff won the eighth it enabled him to get into his stride but I must admit I didn't think I could lose with a lead like that".

I felt on top of the world at having won from such a position and felt good enough to win the next tournament, the Rothmans Grand Prix, until I lost to Steve 9–5 in the semi-finals. Steve was desperate to win a tournament to make him feel less bad about having lost to Dennis in the world final about six months earlier and he played very well. I made a century in the first frame; he made one in the second and he was ahead 5–1. I made it 5–6. Steve made a 95 to go 7–5. The next frame lasted an hour and, if I'd won it, 6–7 wouldn't have been so bad but, once he'd won it, that was more or less it – 9–5. He beat Dennis 10–9 in the final, which finished at

I earned that glass of wine. I was 7–0 down to Jimmy White. I won 12–10 and that's why I'm holding the Goya trophy

2.15 a.m., and we were all up at the crack of dawn to fly to Toronto for the first Canadian Masters which was at last definite after a couple of false starts.

We all travelled together and Dennis, as usual, was the life and soul of the party. When we were waiting at Toronto Airport for the usual questions at immigration he set up the routine beautifully: "When did you turn professional? What is your ranking? Why did you lose in the qualifying competition at Derby in 1932?" Robert made us all feel very poor by wearing a fur coat. As they were grilling him at the immigration counter, Dennis shouted out: "It's all right for you to come into the country, Robert, but your coat's got to go into quarantine for six months".

It felt strange to be playing there in the kind of setting which I'd got used to in Britain but never experienced in Canada. The tournament was played in the studios of CBC, who took a lot of trouble to get everything right. The only trouble was, I didn't feel right. I managed to beat Jimmy White 5–3 but Steve murdered me 8–1 in the semi-finals. Whether this was because I was over-anxious, as the only Canadian in the event, to play specially well, I don't know. I just couldn't produce the form that I wanted to. From snooker's point of view it all went very well. Dennis beat Steve 9–5 in the final, making three centuries in four frames. The viewing figures were excellent and we felt that we had laid the foundation of something good.

Once again, I didn't do very well at Preston. How I hate that place although the Guild Hall is a good arena. I beat Les Dodd and John Parrott and then I lost 9–7 to Willie Thorne. I was 4–3 down at the interval and as I was preparing in the dressing room for the evening session I used the squirter on my hair spray. The trouble was the squirter wasn't where I thought it was so I squirted the spray straight in my eyes. It stung like hell. I could see but my face was all blotchy. I washed all the spray out but every second game I was needing to bathe my face. Willie said on television afterwards that I'd tried all the tactics on him like holding up play by going to the toilet. He said he was just kidding although it didn't sound like it to me. Whatever the reason, I couldn't play as well as I wanted to, even though at 7–7 it was still anybody's match.

It was certainly no disgrace to lose to Willie because he was playing very well around this time and beat Terry Griffiths and Dennis Taylor as well as myself to reach the final. He should have won that, too, because he was 13–8 ahead of Steve going into the final session. It should have been 14–8, but he missed a very easy blue which completely changed the match. Willie only won one more frame.

Willie and I had every chance to beat Steve and Tony Meo in the semi-finals of the Hofmeister World Doubles because we were 4–1 up and also 5–3. At 5–4 we lost a frame when Steve and Tony needed a snooker and eventually we lost 9–6. If Tony could have Steve sat beside him he would win a lot more big matches than he has. When it comes down to it he lacks a shade of confidence in the big situation but he's very cool when he plays with Steve and he doesn't get flustered. They've only lost once in five years and that was when they got snowed under by Higgins and White. And it isn't because Steve does all the work either. In doubles, you've got to play the game for yourself like you normally would. This business of "I'll do the potting and you play the safety" doesn't work.

In the Mercantile Credit Classic I beat Mike Hallett, Tony Meo and Joe Johnson 5–4. Joe was 4–2 ahead and obviously could have beaten me. Three months later he won the world championship. I always rate players just as opponents rather than as world champion material or whatever, even to myself, but my opinion at the time would have been that Joe would just go on being a good player having the occasional good win, but not doing anything special. I turned out to be wrong, although Joe certainly did have trouble once he had won the title in maintaining that kind of form under the pressure expected of him as world champion.

The only thing I can remember about beating Doug Mountjoy 9–6 in the semis was that in the last frame of the afternoon session, which would have made it only 4–3 to me, Doug tried a slow roller on the black and left it hanging over the pocker. He was so annoyed that he went to jab it with his cue to concede the game. He slammed his cue down. His tip came off and it rolled away underneath the seats. I went back to the hotel to have a bath and a nice steak sandwich, leaving Doug down on all fours looking for his tip.

In the other half of the draw Jimmy beat Steve and in the semi-final Rex Williams. I was down 4–3 at the first interval and Jimmy was two minutes late for the evening session. The rules over late arrival are very strictly enforced these days so he was docked a frame. He had had to go back to his hotel to change his suit whereas I'd brought mine with me, figuring that the more rest I could get between sessions the better. This made it 4–4 and I led 8–5 but Jimmy won the last two frames of the day.

I don't remember anything about the final session except the deciding frame at 12–12. I made sure of the blue because that meant that Jimmy needed a snooker. I give Robert's brother, John, 114 start and he knew the shot I should have played on the pink because he played it against me a couple of months later. He had the sense to roll the pink over the corner when I needed a snooker, but I just didn't think that Jimmy could lay a snooker on me and I just played to pot the pink in the middle. Even the way that Jimmy played the snooker was the riskiest possible way you can play that shot but he just missed getting the double kiss and there I was snookered behind the black. It looked a tough escape and, of course, by then I had also realised that I had played the pink all wrong. I played the escape all wrong as well and Jimmy blasted the pink and black in to win.

That was £45,000 to him, £27,000 to me, five ranking points to him, four to me, but the main thing was I was just mad with myself for letting this one slip away. It didn't help when the press couldn't recall Jimmy ever winning a frame before when he needed a snooker.

After all that, I won the Benson and Hedges again. I beat Joe Johnson 5–3 and then Terry Griffiths 5–2 when Terry made a big to-do about the cushions not throwing the right angles. I won the first frame after needing a snooker with only pink and black left. John Street, who was the referee, twice called Terry for a miss because the escape to the pink was, as the regulations say, "not of a standard to be expected of a professional player". Terry was obviously trying his best to hit the pink because it's quite different from the kind of situation where the purpose of the snooker is tactical rather than to gain points.

After the frame, he left the arena for seven minutes and complained about the table. There was something in what he was saying, but to go out for seven minutes as he did was over the top. It wasn't going to do him any good because you can't just pull the table apart there and then and put it together again. It's not going to make me feel bad. It's not going to help him feel good. And in any case, if the cushions were so bad, how had I laid the snookers? Terry's a good guy but sometimes he overreacts.

I beat Tony Knowles 6–4 and then I beat Jimmy 9–5 in the final. The big frame was when I was 6–5, having been 6–3. Jimmy was in with 59 but went in-off and eventually I cleared up with 52 to win on the black which was 8–5, three up with four to play. It isn't the centuries but the 50 to 60 clearances which usually made the difference. Jimmy said afterwards: "Cliff played solid all day. I didn't nick any frames off him but he nicked two or three off me".

It wasn't as dramatic, so they said, as our other two finals that season, the Goya and the Mercantile, but those are the kind of judgments I never make about my own matches. It was a good match, a satisfying result, and there was a sell-out crowd. That was enough for me.

I turned down an invitation to go to Belgium for the Belgian Classic because I wanted to honour a commitment I had made to do a benefit in Toronto for John Ostler, a friend of mine from way back who had smashed himself up in a motor-cycle accident and was paralysed from the waist down. When Barb and I first got together we used to stay for weekends at John and Mary's.

So my next tournament was the Dulux British Open at Derby where I beat Mark Wildman 5–1 and lost in the last 16 to Tony Meo 5–3. Tony had just won the English championship, beating Steve in the semi-finals and Neal Foulds in the final, so he was full of confidence. As with a lot of best of nines, it could have gone either way.

Steve beat Willie in the final and Willie also lost in the Benson and Hedges Irish Masters final to Jimmy after beating me 6–4 in the semis. I had beaten Eugene Hughes the previous day and played quite well. That night, I had eight pints of Guinness. I wasn't playing until the next night so I figured I'd have plenty of time to get over it. Next day, I thought I was going to have a heart attack. My head was thick and I was sweating. I've never had that stuff again. It doesn't bring out the best in me to stay in the same hotel as all the other guys with so much Irish hospitality going on. The Irish are all so friendly that they expect you to be the same way with them. I could do this easily. I would like to do this. As long as I don't have to play snooker. So I guess it's all just a bit too friendly and maybe I'm not much of a country boy at heart because the hotel and the venue, which is a bloodstock sales ring called Goffs, is right out in the middle of nowhere. The venue is fine. The hotel is fine. It's just that I guess that I'm more at home in the cities.

But I did think it was time that I gave some thought to how I was playing Willie because he had now beaten me three out of the last four times we'd played. Willie loves to have some sort of approval vibe coming from somewhere. Above all, he hates to be ignored. I had to play him in the 1986 world championship after I'd beaten Bill Werbeniuk and Eugene Hughes. We were still in the stage of the competition where there are two matches in the arena and the players in each match share the same table for sitting out. This means that you're only a couple of feet apart when you're sitting down between frames. I didn't talk to him at all while we were sat down and I didn't watch him play. Had I learned something? Anyway, I won 13–6 and Willie definitely didn't play as well as he had done in our last few previous matches.

This put me into the semi-finals against Steve, the match which the pundits thought was going to decide the championship. They may have been right, but not in the way they meant because after Steve had beaten me 16–12 he faded out against Joe Johnson in the final, whether because he had used up a lot of reserves against me or not, who can say.

Barry Hearn called the semi-final a match for the purists. The safety was very good, it was very hard fought and there was very little missed. It looked as if I was going to lead 4–2 because I started out with nine reds, eight blacks, 65, in the sixth frame. I was just starting to think about a 147 when I had a kick on the ninth black. Steve cleared up to the pink with 65 and then potted the black to make it 3–3 instead of 4–2 to me. This was obviously good for Steve's morale, not so good for mine. He won the last two frames of that session to make it 5–3. I didn't get level until the first frame of the third session, which I won on the black after Steve had been 62–0. In that session, I went a frame in front three times but never managed to make it two so it was 11–11 going into the final session and then 12–12.

I'd just made a 104 to level so I was feeling pretty confident at the start of the next. I potted a few balls, but as I took the blue into the yellow pocket I knocked the yellow into the middle. As I remember it, Steve made 40 or 50 off that but I see from the frame scores it was 32. Maybe I remember that 32 as being more because it felt significant in my mind, because I was thinking at the time that if I could win that frame for 13–12 the worst that I could be going back to the dressing room at mid-session would be 13–13.

Losing that frame wasn't so bad but I lost the next one as well to go back to the dressing room down 14–12. Normally, if I fade towards the end, there isn't one shot that stands out but this one did.

Like everybody else, I assumed that Steve would win the final, but Joe got inspired to beat Terry Griffiths from three down with four to play in the quarters and just seemed to sense that he could win it. He also seemed to stay down just a bit longer on his shots. His eyebrows were going up and down like crazy as usual, but they seemed to be going up and down for just a bit longer on each shot.

NINE

THE WAY IT IS

PERHAPS I should say at this point that my life was not just an endless succession of snooker matches. I had a lot of friends to enjoy myself with and whenever I could I got on the golf course. I'm fortunate to be able to play golf to a good standard and it's a game that I love now more than snooker. Probably because it's not a job. Maybe I'd think differently if those roles were reversed but I'm not so sure. I've met so many nice people playing golf and I think the professional golfer has the ultimate lifestyle.

I've played with some of the greats in pro-celebrity events and when I played at Gleneagles with Jerry Pate against Lee Trevino and David Soul I was such a nervous wreck that I had a large brandy before I went out there. We took a bus out to the fifth tee and played nine holes. Trevino told me that he has a pool table at home and Jerry said that he had made a lot of money playing snooker in his lunch hours and that he had virtually put himself through college on it. That night I had dinner with Jerry and Jack Lemmon.

I also played with Seve Ballesteros against Trevino and Howard Keel. Seve made a six-footer on the last green for us to win and just as I was leaving the hotel Seve came up to me and said: "I enjoy your game very much. I think that it's a great game. I think you are a very good player." That made my year.

When Marley were sponsoring the pro-celebrity golf I was at a reception when they asked me if I'd like to play golf at St. Andrews.

I said: "Fine, when?"

"Right now."

"Well, where's the car?"

"No, it's not the car, it's the 'copter out there."

There were about seven or eight of us playing. I was with Bruce Forsyth. We took off and we were up to about 1,000 feet. I had never been to St. Andrews – which is the home of golf and all that – and as we started to zoom in on it I started to get a tremendous feeling. We went over the clubhouse and landed a little off to the side. There was a limo waiting to take us straight to the clubhouse where we got changed and straight out on to the tee. It was my honour – my turn to hit – and I stick my tee down into the ground. I'm almost set to play but the chap that I'm with says that I have to wait.

I said: "Why's that?"

He said: "Just wait".

Eventually this voice comes out. It's the starter and he says: "Play away".

We got to one hole which has got these very famous traps. They're called the Dudies or something. There are three traps, right on the fairway and you can't see them. Bruce asked his caddy where it was best to aim and the caddy said: "Straight at the steeple, straight at the steeple". So Bruce hits his best tee shot all day, perfect, straight at the steeple. We walk down the fairway and Bruce's ball is in the bunker. Bruce is fuming.

He says to the caddy: "I thought you said straight at the steeple".

The caddy doesn't bat an eye: "Yes, but you hit it too straight".

I was totally overwhelmed by the atmosphere of it all. I could almost feel ghosts. It was really eerie. We walked across one little bridge that was about 1400 years old. I'd never even touched anything that old.

I was also playing with Ken Bowden, who's a golf writer who's done all Jack Nicklaus's books. As we were standing on the 18th tee the wind was in our face and the hole was about 370 yards. Ken started to tell me about the British Open of 1972 when Doug Sanders missed a two and a half foot put on the last green to win and Nicklaus beat him in a play-off. They had played 72 holes, four rounds, and Ken told me that every round that Nicklaus played he had driven through the green. As I was standing there with a 30 mph wind in my face this seemed impossible and I was still thinking about what Ken had said when I hit a really bad drive. Then Ken just said to me: "Oh, Cliff, I forgot to tell you. Jack had the wind behind him".

I've played quite a bit with Jimmy Tarbuck, Kenny Lynch and Jesus Christ, or at least, Robert Powell. I've also played with all the snooker players. Robert Winsor runs the Snooker Golf Society and we raise money for Robert's pet project, which is buying wheelchairs for handicapped children.

Once I played a four-ball in New Zealand with Willie Thorne, Dennis Taylor and Del Simmons. We had to hire clubs and on the 10th Willie sends his ball 30 feet to the left and his club head about 50 feet to the right. In Toronto, Kirk got so upset once after knocking four balls in a row straight over the fence that he threw his driver up in the air and got it stuck in a tree. It was there for months. Finally, he hits a drive that's okay, but then he dumps two more balls in the water just in front of the green. This is too much for him so he picks up his trolley and bag and throws them in the lake. He storms off, goes 50 yards and comes back. We think he has cooled down but, in fact, he takes his shoes off and throws those in the lake as well.

I've also played under the "free throw" rule which was invented by Des Heather of Jameson Whiskey. As Des explained it, the rule was that he would be entitled to one free throw per round. I agreed to this thinking that he would use it when he was in the rough somewhere. About the fifth hole I chipped up about a foot from the hole. Des picked my ball up and threw it in the middle of bush. Then he explained that that was his free throw.

During the summer I won the Canadian championship again. I beat Jim Wych 6–2 in the final and considering I hadn't played much I played okay. I also went to Hong Kong with the Barry Hearn group for the Hong Kong Masters. There were eight players, Barry's Magnificent Seven and me. We all got along fine and I had a great time, even if it was strange sometimes being asked to autograph group photos when I wasn't even on them. It was good to have the opportunity to see Hong Kong, but the snooker side of it, from my pont of view, was a disaster. Without realising that I was entitled to have an hour on the match table, which was like a US Open green, I practised on some slow tables so when I went into the match I just had no control whatsoever. I lost 3–0 to Willie Thorne in about 40 minutes. The only good thing about it was that it gave Robert a chance to do his Winston Churchill imitation. "Never," he said. "Never in the field of snooker has a man travelled so far and received so much money for doing so little."

After this, Barry invited me to be the eighth man in the Rothmans Matchroom League, which was announced in October and which ran from January to May. At first I was very wary about the whole idea of a league because there had been one in 1984 which had lost about £100,000 with none of the players getting any prize money. Fortunately I didn't play in that one. With leagues, there's always going to be a few matches at the end which don't mean anything though it is an incentive for the players if the prize money runs all the way down the line. A lot of people were very doubtful whether Barry could make a success of it with no television coverage, but with the sponsorship from Rothmans, a lot of local sponsorship and fantastic crowds just about everywhere it was a big success. One place, I played in front of 2,000 people. Most of the venues we used were the kind of places where they don't often see star names from any walk of life so maybe this helped build it up as well. I beat Steve 5–3 at Northampton just before the 1987 world championship, but I ended up finishing seventh with two wins, two draws and three defeats. The margins between any of the players were very small and Steve ended up winning it with four wins and one draw only because Tony Meo won his last frame against Neal Foulds on the black with a 71 clearance. Had Tony missed, Neal would have won it.

Perhaps this is the place to say that Barry has certainly mellowed since I first knew him. I met him first when Steve won the UK in 1980 and Barry walked around with the trophy for about four hours. I figured from that he was seriously into it. I was world champion at the time and Barry invited me down in the February to play Steve in an exhibition at Romford. I was getting £300 which was a good fee at the time, but I thought that we were going to play exhibition snooker. I guess this showed how naive I was because Barry had got just about every leading professional down to Romford to play Steve, and Steve had beaten everybody.

I can remember driving down with Barb. Somehow, she had bought an iron and she was ironing my dress shirt in Barry's office. The match room was crammed and I got a very big cheer when I was introduced. There was a maple leaf flag stuck up in one corner and the Union Jack over in the other. You don't get this at too many exhibitions. Then they played some song which had been written about Steve and then Steve got some fantastic spiel and a reception like you wouldn't believe. The score was 6–0. To Steve. I learnt something there.

Barry was a rougher diamond in those days. He had to win all the time. He had to annihilate people all the time. He behaved as if nobody else existed except him and Steve. I've never been that way in my life. This or that person isn't sat over in that corner dead. He's a walking, talking human being. In the early days, I think Barry got a little carried away. I'm sure he looks back and cringes at one or two of the things he did or said.

But I have to say that in five or six years since then he's changed a lot and he's the most dynamic, well controlled and best organised person there's ever been on his side of the game. He's a pleasure to do business with and Robert and I do quite a lot of business with him. He sets up a deal and he delivers what he promises. He's good company and he keeps his group happy which can't be all that easy when they're all competing so strongly and trying to be the best. He's done lots of good for the players that have been involved with him and also for the game. He thinks big, he presents everything very well and it's obvious he's going to be a major force in the game, particularly overseas because it's Barry who's put a lot of the groundwork in himself. I couldn't see Barry running the game because he's not interested enough in the underdogs, the guys in the lower part of the rankings, but to be fair, he's never pretended to be.

Steve has also changed. When I first knew him I thought he had a very good attitude. Then I think he went through a phase when he was very heavily influenced by Barry. When he stuck his fist up to the crowd and all that it seemed to me that that was Barry not Steve. Some of the things he said were Barry and not him. On the other hand some people took cheap shots at him and there was a lot of professional jealousy, although some of the criticisms were maybe deserved. In the last few years Steve has mellowed and it's been good for him, I think, to be involved in a group of players instead of being the only one. I'm glad that he's found a girlfriend so at least we all know now he's not just thinking about snooker. He's very professional in everything he does, a great ambassador and of course a great player. He's still got tremendous dedication even after winning so much. I don't know that I've got the dedication that he has. I'm not sure that I can play more than three months at a time full out.

Anyway, I started the British season in 1986–7 like I started 1985–6 by winning the Langs Scottish Masters, even though it did involve another set-to with Higgins.

I beat John Parrott 5–1, but he won the first and was 52–0 in the second with me needing a snooker. I won that on a re-spot black and John just faded away. You're bound to lose frames like that a hundred times in your career and you've got to learn not to make a big thing of it. John still gets upset at things like that and it throws him. I'm not counting on it that this will always happen. John has a great technique and a lot of potential and I thought he had a very good attitude when he did well in his first couple of years as a professional. People were quickly building him up as a world champion and he was keeping things in perspective.

Stephen Hendry hadn't been a professional for more than about a year when he said he was going to be world champion within five years. He could because he's a tremendous potter with a lot of ability, but maybe it's time now for John Parrot to be saying or at least thinking this kind of thing whereas Stephen perhaps should have been keeping some of the pressure off himself by saying the kind of thing that John did.

I knew Jimmy White around the same age as Stephen Hendry is now and Jimmy was a better player in my opinion at that age. On the other hand, in matches, Stephen has a bit more sense to his game than Jimmy had. He needs to learn more about playing safe and getting out of snookers, which he's not that good at yet, but he's done amazingly well in his first couple of seasons as a professional and obviously could be a future champion.

In the Langs this time, Jimmy beat Stephen 5–1 and then I beat Jimmy 6–2. I hardly missed anything and Jimmy got a bit frustrated at times. Higgins beat Kirk 6–2 in the other semi-final and then I beat Higgins 9–8 in the final. It was 5–3 to me and then I was 7–5 down. Then we had a very long frame. Near the end of it, the blue was tight on the baulk cushion and Alex was playing from down by the pink. He just tried to nick the blue so that he hardly moved it. I thought he'd missed it. The referee thought he'd missed it too, and gave a foul. I won the game, which made it 7–6 to Alex, but then Alex keeps me sitting in my chair for ten minutes while he takes off to the television scanner wanting to see a replay of whether he'd hit the blue. The frame is over. The referee has made his decision. Nothing is going to change it. So what the hell is he doing except keeping me waiting?

Anyway, I made it 7–7. He went 8–7 and I won 9–8. The last couple of games were a free-for-all because we both started missing. I said in my victory speech that he was a great player to make things a bit easier because I just knew that I was going to have problems with him. Up in the sponsors' room, I'm having a drink with Ted Lowe, who'd been doing the commentary, and Bill Malcolm, who is BBC Scotland's top sports producer, and there are a couple of members of the press stuck round the corner. Alex is fuming because he's lost and brings up the incident about the blue ball. He said he'd hit it and I said he didn't. I mention the incident in the UK at Preston the previous November when the referee hadn't heard me nominate the green and Alex said that this was completely different. It was okay that the referee's decision had been final in the UK but here was Alex saying that the referee's decision wasn't final up in Scotland.

Then he said: "You're lucky" and I said: "Why's that?" He mentioned something about drugs and I said: "What do you mean?" He started to walk around the room and he said: "You know, the bags of white powder". He never actually mentioned cocaine, but this was obviously what he meant. I said: "Listen, you'd better shut up. You're way out of line here. If you don't want me to do the same thing that I've done to you twice before, then don't say anything." So then I go downstairs in the lift with Ted and he says: "Cliff, I don't know how you stood for that." I was waiting for Higgins to come to my door or phone me up and say something, but he didn't.

I guess it would have been over right there except that these guys from the press were in the sponsors' room and heard it all or at least some of it. It came out in the papers and all hell was let loose. The thing that upset me most was that my dad just couldn't understand how I was involved in a story like this. Because he saw sportsmen just as sportsmen my dad thought that Higgins was okay and that there must somehow be something in what he was saying. If this kind of stuff had come from somebody else it would have sounded real bad, but coming from Higgins it just kinda blew over after a while.

All the same, two major companies who I do a lot of work with had to have board meetings to decide whether they wanted to stay with me – BCE and Scottish

Provident. I have a cue contract with BCE and Scottish Provident were using me in company advertising and for company evenings. In fact, the deals which Robert negotiated with BCE, Scottish Provident and Creda were the first serious off-table money I'd ever earned.

I was raging mad at the aggravation all this had caused me and it never occurred to me that I might have to defend myself but suddenly the WPBSA say that I have to go down to Bristol to talk about my lifestyle past and present. We put a stop to that one. Robert put in a complaint on my behalf about Higgins's conduct. A couple of months later Higgins head-butted Paul Hatherell at the Tennents at Preston and grabbed and abused a couple of referees at the Dulux qualifying. Because of all these incidents and, I guess, his previous record, he ended up being fined £12,000 and suspended from five tournaments. I thought he got off easy if anything. Can you imagine what would happen if a top golfer head-butted a golf official? He'd be barred for at least a year, life maybe if he had any kind of bad record.

After the Langs I had intended to go straight to Bristol for the Rothmans qualifying, which is what I should have done, but with all the trouble and aggravation I went home to see Barb. We had come over in the summer and moved into Tony Woodcock's house in North London. I was going to drive from London to Bristol that night to play next morning, but I was just so tired that about 8.30 I lay down on the bed and couldn't wake up. I went down in the morning for the 10.30 start but it wasn't the same. I didn't feel right, I didn't have time to have any practice and I was playing Joe O'Boye, who was good enough to beat me if I gave him too much encouragement. I had lots of chances but Joe played well and kept his head at the end so he beat me 5–4.

Getting knocked out of the Rothmans, having done very well in it for the previous two years felt very strange. It even felt strange while I was playing in the BCE, knowing that I wouldn't be playing in the Rothmans afterwards. I don't really like the system for a lot of the ranking tournaments where you play the qualifying stage in one, then the televised stage in another. I like to play a tournament straight through because it's easier to concentrate that way, staying in the same place, having it in your mind who's ahead of you in the draw and things like that.

Actually, I had played two qualifying matches in the BCE before I'd gone to Scotland for the Langs. I remember my first match against Pascal Burke not because I won 5–0 but because it was Jamie's first day at school. I felt it was a big day in my life, Barb's life and Jamie's life and it was really great to take him in there to start a new stage in his development. I drove up to Derby feeling very relaxed and never missed a ball. I beat Jim Wych 5–3, but when I was 2–0 and 64–0 Jim cleared up with 73 to win the third. He played very well to get back to 3–3 until he started to miss a few near the end.

If anything, I think Jim is a better player now than when he got to the world championship quarter-finals at his first try in 1980. His trouble was that he didn't really want to come over to England full-time which is the only way you can keep improving and become a world class player. He stayed home in Calgary finishing his physical education degree, playing some golf and getting a few things set up and, of course, just playing snooker in fits and starts he lost ground. So even if he is a better player than he was when he first came over the trouble is that everyone else is too. Now that he's committed himself again, Jim is starting to push forward, but he's still got to make the adjustment from playing for fun, which is pretty well what it was in 1980, when everything was a big adventure for him, and seriously playing full time for his living. It was a help to Jim, I think, that he became the second player that Robert manages and by the end of the season Robert had a group of five with Dene O'Kane, Kirk Stevens and Paddy Browne. I like all of them.

The televised stage of the BCE was at Stoke. Even though Goya had pulled out as sponsors to be replaced by BCE, I was, in effect, the defending champion. In my first match on television I had another marathon against Terry Griffiths. I was 4–1 up and won 5–4. In the sixth frame, I scored first with 43 and Terry won it with a 63. In the seventh, he made a very good clearance to tie and then potted the re-spot black. In the eighth, he made another good clearance to win on the black to make it 4–4.

The WPBSA have a rule that no frame can be started less than 40 minutes before the next session is supposed to start so at 4–4 we had to come off. As Terry had just won three on the run he would obviously have preferred to have gone on. I would have been quite happy to go on as well, but having to stop was probably a blessing in disguise for me. We came back for the ninth frame after the evening match had finished and it could have gone either way. Terry needed the pink and black but got the double kiss when he was trying to double the pink and left it over a pocket.

So why do Terry and I always have these long matches? It could be because we play a similar type of game. Terry takes his time and likes to think things out, as I do. We both know, shot for shot, what the other one is going to do. I know that if I play a certain safety he's going to respond in a certain way and so either of us can be planning out the next two or three moves in a way that would be absolutely impossible with a different type of player. I don't think Terry has ever been down to his last dollar playing snooker but he sometimes plays as if he has. I do know that when you are in that situation you don't go for the long deep screw shot knowing that if you miss it you won't have anything left over for your chocolate bar and Coca Cola for supper.

In the quarter-finals, I beat Cliff Wilson 5–1. He is a great one for saying things like: "I'm playing Thorburn today. I'm going to bring a book". Maybe he feels that he can say things like that because he's naturally a very quick sighter and striker, but actually I think that if he's going to bring a book he should read my instructional book because then he might learn something. He's a great potter but he plays as if he's trying to win "Shot of the Tournament". He's gone up to 17th in the rankings which is a good performance, but he could do with being a bit higher yet before he makes the kind of cracks that he does.

I beat Peter Francisco 9–7 in the semi-finals which was a lot closer than perhaps it should have been as I was ahead 6–2. I lost a little concentration and Peter started to play really well. It was 6–6 and then 7–7 and then I won the next two frames with a 116 and a 75. Peter has the makings of being a top player. He pots just as well as Silvino, but he's got more touch and flair. His safety is not bad and when he's trapped he's as good as anyone in the world for knocking in a long ball and screwing right back. Perhaps he needs a bit more self-belief and he will also have to keep working at his game. A lot of good players have forgotten this. After getting to the semi-final and doing so well against me I thought that he would probably get into the top 16 by the end of the season, but he didn't play so well in the last few tournaments.

It's not easy for Peter or for Silvino, who's his uncle, to do what I've done, which is to bring his family over to live in a foreign country. The press don't go that big on us, which in the case of Silvino and myself may be something to do with our style of play, and we don't have any natural source of support that a player playing in his own country usually has. The trouble with snooker is that the pressure tends to build up inside your head. There's no outlet for it like there is in more physical sports.

While I was coming through the top half of the draw, Neal Foulds was coming through the bottom. Steve had a big struggle to beat Rex Williams 5–4 and then lost to Eugene Hughes 5–4. Neal beat Eugene in the semis so he ended up in the final without having to beat one of the top players. For this reason, he was just a bit fresher than perhaps he would have been if he'd had to play a long match with Steve.

I'd known Neal since he was about 14. He wore enormous glasses and he was just Geoff's son, Geoff being the London amateur champion round that time and one of the best amateurs in the country. Nobody then thought Neal would ever make it. He wasn't all that good and there were so many good young players around, but I do remember, now that I come to think about it, that wherever I saw Geoff in those days I saw Neal practising. He's spent all his life in a very snooker-orientated type of environment and he has just kept at it. Geoff says that Neal's game improved virtually overnight when he started wearing contact lenses so this has obviously been a factor. Geoff has been very good for Neal in talking snooker with him, advising him and steadying him for his matches, but now Geoff has sat through so many of Neal's matches that Neal should start steadying Geoff.

My main impression of the final is of Neal knocking in all sorts of long pots and screwing back 10 feet if he felt like it. His long potting was so good that he almost always got in first. I see that *Snooker Scene* reported that he was ahead in 13 of the 14 frames on the first day, but it was only 7–7 overnight. That day, I won five frames on the black and another on the pink. In the last but one frame I was 40 behind with one red left. I won this for 7–6 and then Neal won the last.

I'd felt my tip getting hard in the semi-final and of course as the final went on it felt even worse. I decided to stay with it for the final session the next afternoon rather than try to play with another one but after a few frames I just felt that there was no way I could win unless I took a chance and changed it. Neal was ahead 9–7. I won the next but only because Neal had played badly. There was no way he was going to keep on playing like that so I asked for the 15 minutes time out, which the WPBSA rules allow, to change my tip. For two frames the new tip felt so different that I couldn't play with it so at 11–8 I was three down with four to play. I played well in the next and thought that Neal might feel a bit of pressure as he got near the winning post for his first professional title. Some of his touch did go, but he still potted well and he won the next frame to win it 12–9.

This was the start of a great season for Neal. He went from 13th to third in the world rankings, edging me down to fourth and he's obviously got a lot of good years ahead of him. I felt quite frustrated to lose the BCE final because of the problem that I had had with my tip. In that kind of situation there's always that niggling feeling that something beyond your control has stopped you giving of your best.

Actually it was a bad season for that kind of feeling because I had tip trouble again in the world championship and I was ill when I lost in two other ranking tournaments. I don't like to make excuses but it did seem to me a little strong that in four ranking tournaments out of six something happened which made it nearly impossible for me to play to my normal standard right through.

It was very frustrating after the BCE to sit around at home while everybody else was playing in the Rothmans at Reading. I like to be where the action is and it felt very flat just practising and doing ordinary things. At that time I was renting a house from Tony Woodcock, the footballer. It was a lovely house but we had about two-thirds his furniture and about a third our own. It was good but it wasn't quite home and I was paying a lot of money to rent it. Barb and I wanted our own house and now that we've got it we're very happy there but at this time we didn't feel settled. We must have looked at about 110 homes and that wears you out too. It was January 1987 before we bought our present house.

Not being involved in the Rothmans, I wanted to go to Toronto for the Canadian Masters a week early, rather than go with the rest of the boys the day after the Rothmans finished. I was told that if I did this I would have to buy my own ticket. As I like to go either first class or Club that would have cost me about £1,500 so I decided to go out with the group. That was when I discovered that three of the other players had gone two days earlier, which would have suited me much better because I could have met up with most of the friends I had in Toronto who wanted to see me and perhaps got down to some proper practice before the tournament.

A couple of hours after I check into the hotel in Toronto – which again is a strange feeling considering it used to be my home town – I'm sat there at a press conference and I'm told two minutes beforehand that I have to stand up and greet the players. This is not a really big deal, but I can do without public speaking. I was struggling with my game and I didn't want any more pressures, however small. The first couple of nights I was there at the hotel the phone never stopped ringing. I phoned down to stop the calls but they kept coming through. Finally I went downstairs at two o'clock in the morning and spelt it out that no more calls meant no more calls. Tony Knowles beat me 5–1 and I played poorly.

A couple of days after I got back to London I had to play in the Dulux qualifying at Solihull against Mark Wildman. I drove up there nice and easy and I've got so much time that I even go for a drive round town. At five after two I show up and there's a guy standing outside the hall saying "Hurry, hurry". Robert had the match down on my booking sheet as 3 o'clock whereas in fact it should have been 2 o'clock. I just accepted that I'd lost the first game for late arrival and tried to relax. I won 5–2, so with the frame forfeit, it was 5–3.

From there, I went to Blackpool for the qualifying stage of the Mercantile Credit Classic. I made 112 and 140 in the last two frames against Graham Cripsey, but I lost in the next round to Dean Reynolds 5–4. I was starting to go under with flu, but, more important than that, I didn't think much of the referee we had. I thought Dean should have been called for a "miss" three or four times because any referee who understood anything about the kind of snooker we play would have known that Dean was much more concerned with leaving the white safe than getting out of the snooker. Incidentally, I would not have anyone refereeing championship snooker who could not make, or at least could make not too long ago, a 50 break.

I'd got over this flu by the time I played Danny Fowler in the Tennants UK at Preston. I made a 109 break in the first frame and a 119 in the second which wasn't bad for ten in the morning but I was down 7–5. Danny is a very good player and practises a lot with Bill Werbeniuk at Worksop, where Bill has been based for a few years now. I had seen him play Steve in the Rothmans and get into a position to win several games. He usually lost them through taking on tough shots and playing them in such a way that if he misses he's more or less bound to lose the game. He did this a couple of times against me and he also faded a bit near the end. I won 9–7 but I knew I had been in a match.

I went back home and Barb, who had caught the flu from me, I think, gave it right back to me. It crossed my mind that Steve never gets the flu but this is probably because he takes better care of himself. It took a while for it to come out in me for the second time because I beat David Taylor 9–4 and John Spencer 9–2, but by the time I played Neal Foulds in the quarter-finals I could hardly lift my arms up. I was shaking, sweaty and streaming with cold. I was down 6–1 at the interval. I made a 125 in the first frame at night, but Neal was playing very, very well and wrapped it up 9–2. I then spent the next two days in bed. Steve beat Neal in the final.

Willie and I beat Jim Wych and Dene O'Kane in the Hofmeister World Doubles and then lost to Mike Hallett and Stephen Hendry 5–4. Mike and Stephen just went for everything. They had a great week and beat Neal Foulds and John Parrott in the quarters and John Virgo and Kirk Stevens in the semis before Davis and Meo beat them easily in the final. Doubles is a very strange game. I liked Kirk's comment after one of the matches he and Virgo won: "John did the potting *and* the safety. I was just somebody for him to talk to."

Losing in the qualifying of the Mercantile meant that I had no more tournament play until the Benson and Hedges Masters at the end of January. The fewer matches you have, the more you have to feel your way. I beat Rex Williams 5–1 and Willie Thorne 5–3 and lost 6–5 to Dennis Taylor in the semi-finals. Dennis and I started at noon and finished at 5.50. Apparently someone asked why Dennis was wearing evening dress and the reply was that it was because he had come prepared to play all night. I love these jokes about long matches.

Dennis was ahead 5–4 and I had to clear to the pink with 50 to make it 5–5. Dennis looked a bit demoralised, as if he thought he had missed his chance, and I also thought that I was going to win the decider. When I took the last red it put me 23 in front, but it was a straight pot down the side rail so I couldn't get the cue ball away from the cushion. I just played to roll the black in, which would have put me 30 in front. I'd missed quite a few shots from the cushion in this match and I missed this one so this meant that Dennis could still win with all the colours. He played safe from the yellow and half-snookered me. I left him a chance from this and Dennis knocked the colours in to win on the black. In all the years that he'd been playing in the Masters, Dennis had only won one match before this week so I guess he was due for a good run. I had only needed the one ball to beat him in the semi-finals and Higgins was in the same position in the final but Dennis beat him from three down with four to play. Afterwards Dennis said: "Alex played as if he was Cliff Thorburn. I haven't seen him play better for some time. I expected him to lash out, but he refused those sort of shots."

My next tournament was the Dulux British Open at Derby. Graham Cripsey, who I'd beaten 5–0 in the Mercantile, played quite a bit better this time and I won

5–2. I had to win the last two frames to beat Doug Mountjoy 5–4. Doug has just won the Welsh championship and was playing pretty well, but I think he felt the pressure in the last couple of frames because he had never beaten me. In fact, when I think of it, I haven't lost to a Welshman for about five years.

The bookmakers had me 5–1 on to beat David Taylor, but they didn't know that I had tonsillitis. The antibiotics I was having to take were making me feel a little drowsy and I hadn't felt like practising. So I decided I wouldn't take any pills until the match was over. They might have been good for my health but they weren't going to help me to win. After two frames my highest break was ten. In the third frame I made a 19, but David won this, too. I started to pick up and made it 3–3. I won the sixth after needing a snooker. In the seventh, David scored 87 and lost, which has got to be the only time this can ever have happened in professional snooker. I won the frame 90–87. He made a 61 and I needed two snookers. I thought a couple of times about giving up, but eventually I got the snookers and won the game on the black. By now I felt really rough but I had a large brandy and somehow I won the next as well to win 5–3.

I had three days off before I played Jimmy White in the semi-finals. Again I didn't take the pills on the day of the match. In the afternoon, I felt absolutely tremendous. It was 4–3 to me at the interval. At night, I just felt very, very tired, just like I had felt against David Taylor. The brandy didn't work this time. Jimmy made a couple of centuries and beat me 9–5. Then he beat Neal in the final.

The Belgian Classic was cancelled and the world cup looked doubtful for a time. There were sponsorship problems with both these events and it even looked for a time as if the world cup was not going to be for countries, which was the whole point of it, but for teams of three just picked from the ranking list. As the No 2 in the ranking list, I would have played with a Welshman, Ray Reardon, who was 15 and John Campbell, an Australian, who was 18. The idea was that each team's rankings would add up to 35. The whole idea was ridiculous and eventually we played with the usual countries system. We beat England in the semi-finals but Ireland beat us 9–2 in the final.

Dennis beat me 5–1 in the Irish Masters which meant that in five appearances I had won only two matches in that event. Steve powered through everybody that week and some of the papers got very excited about what they thought was a betting coup. It turned out that what happened was that someone had a big bet on Tony Meo to beat Tony Knowles and the money kept being laid off by one bookmaker to another all over the country. Of course, all these bets were on Meo so the rumour was that the match was fixed. It was absolutely ridiculous, of course, and the bookmakers must have been looking for publicity or just not prepared to pay up when they lost. People don't realise what you have to do to become a professional snooker player. You have to work your butt off and to think that anybody would throw that away for a few hundred pounds is just a joke. Anybody who knows anything about the inside of professional snooker knows that winning is everything.

Although everything had seemed to go wrong in the big tournaments I felt very confident in the two or three weeks before the world championship. I was making five or six centuries a day on the table at Robert's house, which is tighter than the ones we play the tournaments on and the day before the championship I made a 147. Dene O'Kane had played really well in the qualifying to come through his

Team Snooker: Ireland beat us in the final of the World Cup in 1986. Alex Higgins, Eugene Hughes, Dennis Taylor did it for them. Bill Werbeniuk, Kirk Stevens and myself couldn't quite do it for us

section so that he played me in the first round at Sheffield. Because Dene was in our group and I had got to know him quite well I wanted him to play well at Sheffield but obviously not too well. We practised together pretty well every day, but because he was skint the deal was that if I won I wouldn't get anything but if he won I gave him a tenner.

At the Crucible everything was fine for the first five frames. My safety was good. I was potting well. I felt really solid. Dene was struggling to adapt to the conditions at the Crucible and also the pressures. Just as I was winning the sixth frame to make it 5–1 my tip split. I had to turn the cue over so that I was playing with the weak side of the tip and soon I knew and Dene knew that when I played with side I had no control at all. I couldn't believe that this had happened to me and I also knew very soon I was in trouble. Dene made a 52 break in the next frame and won the one after that on the black, which was probably very important as it would have given me a bit of a breathing space at 6–2. Instead, by winning this frame and the last, Dene was behind only 5–4.

I put a new tip on straightaway and practised with it that night for two hours plus four hours the next day, but when I got back in the arena it still felt like a new tip. Everytime I struck the cue ball off centre I felt I had no control. Dene had himself well psyched up and made a 91 in the first frame and a 90 in the second. That put him ahead 6–5 and when he won the next on the black it was all over. I kept trying but I felt as if I had nothing to try with. Dene played well, very well and took his chance in a way that not everybody in his kind of position would have done. He beat Doug Mountjoy as well to get to the quarters and Steve won the championship.

For me, it was a disappointing end to a disappointing and frustrating season. In four of five tournaments, things had happened to me – illness, tip trouble – which all had serious effects. I'm a much better player than I ever was, even if at certain times a particular kind of hardness wasn't there. I have to put it down as a real bad year, but I still had chances to win four or five tournaments and 123 other players would have liked to have done as well as I did. I'm happier than I've ever been in my life and Barb and I are so much more settled where we are now than out at Walton-on-Thames where we were in 1980 and 1981.

We've more friends and we love London, but there's no way I would want to live in England if I was playing at a lower standard. If I'm not going to be playing very well I'd rather be back home but actually I think that with the snooker brain I've got I can last longer than most players. I'll know before most people when it's time to quit. I couldn't show up just to get some money for losing in the first or second round. I'd rather be involved in a snooker club or something like that. When the right time comes I'd like to be involved with a group of young kids and perhaps bring them over to play the tournaments and be a father figure to them and all that. I would get satisfaction out of that and I don't think I'd have any trouble using up any spare time I had on the golf course. Tony Johnstone, a golf pro from Zimbabwe said to me while we were playing together in a pro-am: "Cliff, it must be so tough for you. You play the two biggest mind and mental games there are." It's just lucky I'm in love with both of them.

TEN

A SNOOKER WIFE'S
POSTSCRIPT

IN CLIFF AND BARB's lounge in their home in Arkley, at the Hertfordshire corner of North London, is a wooden plaque presented by a grateful parent whose seven-year-old son began his year in Barb's class of 35 mixed infants very troubled and ended it confident and happy. The words on this plaque, the parent said, exemplified her enlightened approach as a teacher and perhaps hint at some of the qualities – in contrast to some of his negative early influences – which drew Cliff to her and made him confident that his children would never have to cope with the early psychological handicaps which he had to struggle so hard to overcome. The words read:

> If a child lives with criticism, he learns to condemn;
> If a child lives with hostility, he learns to fight;
> If a child lives with ridicule, he learns to be shy;
> If a child lives with shame, he learns to feel guilty;
> If a child lives with tolerance, he learns to be patient;
> If a child lives with encouragement, he learns to feel confidence;
> If a child lives with praise, he learns to appreciate;
> If a child lives with fairness, he learns justice;
> If a child lives with security, he learns to have faith;
> If a child lives with approval, he learns to like himself;
> If a child lives with acceptance and friendship, he learns to find love in the world.

This postcript to Cliff Thorburn's story is about – and by – his wife Barbara.

I was the third of six children, the second eldest girl. We lived in Montreal. I went to the education department of McGill University and I was a teacher for nine years. My father was a chef until he crippled his hand in an accident. Then he did various jobs, but he could never be a nine-to-five man. Cliff is like him in many ways. My father would get some ideal in his head and go out after it. He went bankrupt three times and finally he was a union negotiator.

I'm a very organised person, on time and ordered, and my father and Cliff are anything but. My father liked to drink and play cards and just go off somewhere and not always phone to say where he was. There were many times when I knew that my mother was struggling for money. I guess my father didn't like to feel tied down. Cliff also likes to feel he can go where he wants when he wants. He does phone me but if he says he'll be home at seven I don't expect him to be there much before nine.

My first husband, Paul, was as different from my father as you could get and Cliff is as near. Paul was a college instructor and a half-hour after his last class for the day he would be home. I wouldn't have married him if he hadn't been a nice guy but we just grew apart. The biggest factor was that he didn't want children and I did. Paul was very, very keen on snooker and I met Cliff first of all when Paul and I went to the Canadian championship in 1974. I saw Cliff a few times here and there, but it was all over between Paul and me when we first got together in 1979. When we split up I went back home to live with my mom and dad – at the age of 29. Then my father was dying of cancer and I helped take care of him in his last few months. This was a very emotional time, but it was an experience I was glad to have had.

With Cliff's history, he could have grown up to be a woman-hater, but he was very affectionate and didn't hide it and he was also very, very good with my mom and with my brothers and sisters. As I was in Montreal and Cliff was in Toronto, I took leave of absence in June 1979 which meant that I had to decide whether to give up teaching by the following April. I was sure of Cliff but I just gave myself these few months to decide as a kind of safety net. I was heartbroken to give up teaching, but Cliff couldn't give up snooker and he couldn't move to Montreal.

The first couple of years with Cliff were very exciting. I enjoyed travelling with him, particularly coming to England for the first time. My mother was actually born in London. She was a war bride. It was great to be with Cliff when he won the championship and, of course, it's easy to say now it was a mistake for us to leave Canada then and live at Walton-on-Thames. I felt he was rather pushed into it. I thought maybe he could have stayed in Canada.

I didn't know a soul. I can't say I wasn't desperately lonely at times. The first year wasn't so bad. Cliff was world champion and was still playing quite well. Kirk was living with us. Dinner was always fun. If Cliff was away playing, Kirk was often around and was someone to talk to. I had Jamie, but I had never been around a baby for any length of time before so this was a big adjustment for me. At home, I had never had much to do with my younger sister or two brothers when they were babies. My elder sister was the one who helped my mom in those situations. Other than the health visitor and one friend who moved in down the road, I had no one to communicate with in these areas. Cliff was away playing most of the time. Often I felt very alone and in that frame of mind I didn't help Cliff.

Cliff got more and more unhappy. In the second year we were there, he wasn't world champion. He was losing all the time and this was making him even more unhappy. I realised it was really bad when he wouldn't get out of bed in the morning to play golf. In November 1981, I went home for a few weeks. On the day that Cliff was playing Tony Meo in the Coral UK at Preston I was saying to my mom that if Cliff lost he would come on the phone and say we should come back to Canada. The phone rang. He'd lost. He said: "I can't take this any more. I've got to come home".

So at the end of that season, we came back. The June, July and August were wonderful. I just put out of my head any thought that it would all come to an end when it was time for Cliff to go back to England for the next season. The shock of him leaving, knowing he was going for at least nine weeks, was very hard. It was very hard on Jamie because Cliff doted on him and suddenly daddy wasn't there. I couldn't even pick the phone up to speak to him just whenever I felt like it.

I'm basically a loner. I enjoy being by myself up to a certain point but the routine of just cleaning the house and walking Jamie to the park and nothing else really did get to me. I was in Toronto, 350 miles from my family and the friends I had in Montreal. The only people I knew were Cliff's friends and I felt I didn't want to impose myself by ringing up their wives. Then Cliff would ring up and ask me what I had been doing that day and I would say: "Nothing".

When Cliff was home the next summer, things improved. He loved to have his friends over. I got to know their wives. Some of them I felt I could call up or even go to their houses. When Cliff was away, some would make a point of inviting me over to a barbecue or whatever. Things also improved when Jamie went to nursery school because I got to meet some of the other mothers and made some friends of my own.

I thought I would go back to teaching when Jamie was a little older. My idea was that when he was five I would get a job in the school where he was. I had two miscarriages and I thought I would probably never have another baby. With my second miscarriage, I was on my own and I had to get myself to the hospital. Cliff wanted another baby as much as I did. He felt he had missed so much of Jamie's early years and he also didn't want Jamie to be the only child the way he had been. But I was quite resigned to it and I got so tired and fed up through being in hospital for all the tests.

I got pregnant again in 1985. I had to have tests to show whether everything was okay and I had to wait three weeks for the results. At the start of that season Cliff won the Langs and the Goya, but he was just so miserable through being away for so long. He was doing so well that he was getting to finals and semi-finals all the time so he couldn't fly home, which is what he had been doing previously. Once he came home for five days, which was hopeless. He knew he didn't have enough time. He was tired and he couldn't relax because be knew he'd got to fly back to England so soon.

So I flew over to be with him in November 1985 while I was waiting for the results of the tests. I was nervous about this and I was also not very satisfied with the kind of lives we were leading. We sat up one night until 6 a.m. discussing everything but it all boiled down to one choice: Cliff couldn't give up what he was doing. In any case, snooker wasn't just his living; it was his life. So I said that Jamie and I would move over and we'd buy a house near London.

I went back to get the results of the tests. These were fine. We ruled out Cliff coming home for Christmas because it would have meant him flying home Christmas Eve and flying back New Year's Eve, so Jamie and I came over to England again for Christmas which we spent with Willie and Fiona Thorne. Andrew was born on April 29, 1986.

At first we rented Tony Woodcock's house because by then he was playing for a club in Italy and then we moved to our own house in March 1987. It's in a very nice area with some lovely people. We've been invited to some parties and it's just completely different to how it was at Walton-on-Thames. I see Cliff on a day-to-day basis, which is something I haven't done for four years. He does go away but it's usually just for a few days or for a couple of weeks, not months on end. I'm careful what I tell Cliff when he's away playing. Jamie was in hospital once and they suspected he had cystic fibrosis. It was the third time he had been that way and he had all the symptoms but it turned out that he was okay. I didn't tell Cliff what was suspected. He couldn't have done anything about it and he would just have worried so much he wouldn't have been able to concentrate on his snooker as he needs to.

Moving over from Canada and then moving house has been a lot of upheaval but we're settled now and it's the best situation we've ever had.